Thomas Macfarlane

To the Andes

Being a Sketch of a Trip to South America

Thomas Macfarlane

To the Andes
Being a Sketch of a Trip to South America

ISBN/EAN: 9783337149291

Printed in Europe, USA, Canada, Australia, Japan

Cover: Foto ©Andreas Hilbeck / pixelio.de

More available books at **www.hansebooks.com**

TO

THE ANDES;

BEING A SKETCH OF

A TRIP TO SOUTH AMERICA;

WITH OBSERVATIONS BY THE WAY ON

THE FAMILY, THE CHURCH AND THE STATE,

BY

THOMAS MACFARLANE.

Toronto:
BELFORD BROTHERS.
1877.

TO

JOSEPH WHARTON, Esq.,

OF PHILADELPHIA,

IN WHOSE INTEREST AND AT WHOSE EXPENSE MY

JOURNEY TO SOUTH AMERICA

WAS UNDERTAKEN,

THIS BOOK IS MOST RESPECTFULLY

Dedicated

BY

THE AUTHOR.

PREFACE.

A PREFACE should rather be called a "Prefix," for, in the most of cases, it is written *after* the work to which it is attached. Such, at least, is the case with this introduction, which is, at the same time, an apology for the appearance of the present book.

In the spring of last year it was my good fortune to be asked to undertake certain professional work in New Granada and Ecuador; countries whose names had been in my mind associated with all that is sublime in mountain scenery, luxuriant in tropical vegetation, and interesting in volcanic phenomena, and which, moreover, had been rendered classic ground by the labours of some of the foremost scientific men of the present century. I very willingly engaged to do the work in question, and, while detained in Guayaquil attending to it, took the opportunity of crossing the Western Cordillera of the Andes, principally in order to pay my respects to those ancient mountain monarchs whose names I remembered from my school boy days. I did not anticipate that I would be able to obtain anything beyond the most distant introduction to Chimborazo and the other elevated peaks in its proximity, or that my geological observations, taken by themselves, would be of such a character as to justify me in bringing them prominently before the public. But I afterwards reflected that I had succeeded in viewing the magnificent precincts of these mountains, situated in the most elevated volcanic territory 'n the world, and had become acquainted with the views the book; in order to the easier detection of which, it may here be mentioned that, besides treating of other matters, Chapters I., II., IV. and V. will be found to contain special allusions to family, church, state and nation respectively. Chapter III., which refers more particularly to the scenery and volcanoes of the Andes, may be regarded as the nucleus, to which I have already referred, of my narrative. I confess that in writing the latter I have been influenced by a desire to render it acceptable to a wider circle and a greater variety of readers than is usually commanded by purely scientific writing; and I have endeavoured, in relating my experiences and moralising thereon, to do so in such a manner as may induce the reader to accompany me, in the spirit, with interest and curiosity, "to the Andes."

Staneybrae,
Actonvale, Quebec;
Easter, 1877.

CONTENTS.

CHAPTER I. ACROSS THE CONTINENT.

The Boundary Line—Protection and Free Trade—Start from Montreal—Stockraising—Sunday Travelling—The Hudson River—New York to Omaha—Material Progress in the United States—Young America—Start from Omaha—Travelling Companions—Nebraska and the Plains—The Rocky Mountains—Geological Comparisons—Laramie Plains—The Black Hills and the Indian—American Theory and Practice—Christianity and Civil Government—Along the Watershed—Canons and Gulches—Early Settlement of Utah—Mormons and their Promised Land—The Pilgrim Fathers and the Israelites—Ogden—Bodily Training—Nevada—Mining and Farming—Over-protection—The Sierra Nevada—Descent to Sacramento—Fertility of California—Wheat, Fruit and Precious Metals—Cause of American Material Progress—San Joaquin Valley—Oakland and San Francisco—Social Corruption—"Hoodlums"—The Chinese Question—Home Training and Spiritual Culture—The Warning of Moses.. 1-33

CHAPTER II. THE PACIFIC COAST.

The "Montana"—The Unpacific Ocean—Fellow-passengers—My Spanish Master—Goethe on Woman's Safeguard—Lower California—Chinamen—Sunday the on Pacific—Secular Education—*Deutsche Treue*—Mexico—Administration of Justice—"Woman's Eye"—Acapulco—The Mexican Question—Religious Discipline in Norway—Free Trade in Education—American Parents—Discipline on the "Montana"—Guatemala—Woes and Wars of Central America—*Deutsche Burschen*—Costa Rica—Turtles and Turtle-doves Scepticism—Panama—Parting—The Constellations—The "Croya"—Sunday on the South Pacific—San Buenaventura

—The Andes—Tumaco—Pizarro and his followers—Esmeraldas—Side Hatches—Education again—The Equator—Manta—The Cordillera Cajas—Guayaquil—Payta—Shipping Cattle—Callao—Peruvian Finances—Railways in Peru Religion—Political Fete—Protestantism in Callao—Return Northward 34-70

CHAPTER III. THE CORDILLERAS.

Guayaquil—Dr. Theodor Wolf—The Guayaquil River—Bodegas—On Muleback—Travelling Companions—Tropical Forests—Palmar—Corduroy Mud—Playas—Comfortless Quarters—Native Travellers—The Boulder Region—Orange Groves—Palsabamba—Zig-zag Mountain Paths—Puzo—A Moonlit Morning—Scaling the first Ridge—An Andean Valley—Chapacoto—The Heart of the Andes—Guaranda—Altercation—"Gringo"—*Quebradas*—Pauza—The Chimborazo Pass—The First Amazon Tributary—Tortorillas—Chimborazo—The Eastern Cordillera—Capac Urcu—Central Andean Valleys—Riobamba—The Cerro Ygualata—Carihuirazo—Mocha—The Valley of Ambato—Magnificent Scenery—Cotopaxi—Its Eruptions—Tunguragua—The Lava of Banos—Reiss and Stubel—Quartz in Andean Lavas —Ambato—Earthquakes.. 71-101

CHAPTER IV. ECUADOR.

The Church in Ambato—The Hotel—Muleteers—Stonepicking—Character of the Ecuadorians—Rock Specimens—Scheerer's Satire on Geologists—Llamas—Andean Agriculturists—Chimborazo—Rock Exposures—Indians and Muleteers—General "Twentymiles"—Guaranda again—Ecuadorian Troops—Peasants—The Sun in Ecuador—Northern Summer Eves—Puzo—The Planter of Playas—Bottomless Roads—Savaneta—Return to Bodegas—English Companions—Garcia Moreno—The Jesuits—"Twentymiles" again —The Aborigines—Back to Guayaquil—Sanitary Matters—Geology of Ecuador—Limitless Fields for Scientific Investigation—The Priests—Church and State—British Residents—Disadvantages of a Tropical Country.............. 102-132

CHAPTER V. HOMEWARD BOUND.

The "Islay"—Departure from Guayaquil—Mr. Bullethead—His Scepticism—" Indian Governments "—Peruvian Politics—Missions—Panama—The Isthmus—"Jamaica Niggers"—Aspinwall or Colon—A Perplexed Gambler—The Steamer "Andes"—Caribbean Sea—Navasa—The Windward Passage—Fellow Passengers—The Church of Rome—The Source of Civil Authority—*L'Eglise, c'est moi*—The Husband of the Church — San Salvador — Education in Germany — The Church in Prussia—Vaticanism—Home Rule in Church Matters — Chess — The Church of England — Lessing—Nathan the Wise—New York—Philadelphia—The Centennial Exhibition — Ecuador again — Norway — The National Reform Association—The Bible in the Common Schools—The Duty of the Clergy in Matters of Education—Church and State in Norway—The Scottish Education Act—Return to Montreal—The Good Land—The Duty of Canadians—Victoria, by the Grace of God, Queen, Defender of the Faith..133-174

I.—ACROSS THE CONTINENT.

"My power and the might of mine hand hath gotten me this wealth."
Deuteronomy vii, 17.

It has very frequently occurred to me that few travellers can possibly have passed from Canada into the United States without remarking the transition from inertness to activity, from neglect to idleness, which is apparent at so many points in crossing the boundary line. I do not refer to those who have made the passage so often as to have become familiar with the change, and oblivious to the differences plainly observable, but to those passengers who, like myself, have fewer opportunities of visiting the United States, and whose faculties for observation are, therefore, more on the alert. Who, among the latter class, has, for instance, failed to notice how unfavorably St. Johns contrasts with St. Albans, Prescott with Ogdensburg, Windsor with Detroit, and Fort William with Marquette; or who has passed from New Brunswick into Maine, from the Eastern Townships into Vermont, from the neighbourhood of Kingston into northern New York, from the District of Algoma into the northern peninsula of Michigan, without being struck with the increased life and energy everywhere discernible on the other side of the line, owing to the presence of a more pushing population, or their greater resources and more flourishing manufactures.

I had another opportunity for observing the same differences on the 18th of March, 1876, when I left Montreal for New York on a journey of several thousand miles towards southern latitudes. On that occasion also I was reminded that the differences in question were often considered to be the effects of the respective tariff policies of the two countries, and the temptation within me was strong to reflect upon the merits of the rival theories of free-trade and protection, for discussions concerning them were beginning to agitate the Dominion. But it occurred to me that, after all, absolute free-trade and absolute protection have neither of them any existence on the face of the globe. Great Britain derives an enormous revenue from import duties, and the United States tariff, however "protective," was so arranged in order to provide sufficient income to meet the interest on the enormous war debt. Any difference in principle between the two schools of political economists seems only to exist in the views they entertain as to the duty of the state or government in the matter. The free-traders preach "non-interference," a "*laissez faire*" policy; while the protectionists are more positive, and advocate such action on the part of the state as will provide for the material welfare of the subject; and surely the latter principle would appear to be the correct one. Material prosperity is to the nation what the nourishment of the body is to the individual. It is the foundation of society, without which culture and higher development becomes impossible; just as mind and heart are neither vigorous nor virtuous if the body be neglected. As well might the individual neglect to attend to his physical wants, or refuse to control his animal passions, as the state decline to watch over and legislate concerning commerce, trade and manufactures, in such a manner as to draw from them the greatest amount of material benefit for the community.

When I started on my journey, Montreal was in winter quarters, and the St. Lawrence motionless. Old mother earth lay fast asleep beneath her snowy mantle as we hurried past Laprairie and St. Johns. At St. Albans I encountered the "Chinese wall," of which so much had been said in political discussions, and entered the "flowery land," which name the States might deserve from the thousands of labourers and tradesmen from old Europe who have there found comfort and prosperity. My fellow-travellers, who were mostly Canadians, were inclined to be taciturn, but, fortunately, the bustle of inspecting baggage, and hurriedly swallowing refreshment at St. Albans, had knocked a few of them against each other and effected their introduction. When we afterwards settled down in the sleeping car, I found myself opposite a Montrealer, with whom I had a previous slight acquaintance, while an Ontario farmer, bound for New York, esconced himself beside me. My recent cogitations on protection had impregnated me with that subject, somewhat in the same manner as a Leyden jar carries electricity, and the approach of an appropriate material was alone required to produce a discharge. The Montrealer was an importer, and a liberal, while the man of Ontario was a free-trader and a "grit." Their ideas soon came into contact with those of my surcharged cranium, and the detonation followed, and brisk conversation reverberated until the ordinary stock of arguments on both sides was exhausted. The Montrealer tried to sum up by saying:

"Depend upon it, there's nothing like hard pan. Let's "have no bolstering up of rotten manufactures. Whatever "businesses can't stand on their own legs had better be "allowed to topple over."

"According to your plan," I said, "the little baby that "cannot yet toddle shouldn't receive the slightest assistance "in trying to walk."

"O, never mind babies," said he; "what I mean to say

"is, that a business must pay on its own merits or be abandoned."

"That's a little too sweeping," I maintained. "Many businesses are carried on which do not, at every moment, pay; and there is one in which almost the whole of us are engaged, and in which we are sure to sink money."

"Not if I know it! But you are not serious; you are getting up a conundrum."

"I am quite serious, but I will put it in the form of a riddle if you like. What business is it which is essential to the existence of the human race, is carried on by great numbers in every community, and yet does not pay?"

"I give it up."

"I'll tell you. *Raising a family.*"

"By Jove! I'm in that business myself. But you're right; human stock raising does not pay."

"Well," struck in the Upper Canadian, "I'm in that business too, but I have a better opinion of it. Without my family I could not make my farm pay."

"I'm afraid," said the Montrealer, "your books, if you kept them properly, would tell a different story."

"I can tell pretty well how things are going, without books; and I know that if I had to pay for all the help I get from my family, I should soon get sold out of house and home."

"Perhaps," I interposed; "it all depends on how the business is conducted. I maintain that if as much attention were given to the production and rearing of the human species as is devoted to the breeding and raising of cows and horses, no one would require to complain of being burdened with a large family."

"You're about right," said the farmer. "What sort of animals would we have, and where would be the profit "in raising them, if they were to be fed as luxuriously and "worked as tenderly as boys and girls are now-a-days?"

This question opened a new and interesting subject, which was not exhausted till the train reached Burlington, when we thought it was about time to turn into our berths.

We missed the connection at Troy, but were not obliged to stay over, even although it was Sunday morning. Sunday travelling is much more common in the States than in Canada, and the accommodation of the better classes seems to be especially studied. A fast train left at 8 A.M., in which I soon found myself rolling along the Hudson River. I felt somewhat conscience-stricken, wondered what the Puritan fathers would have thought, and mused on the change which seems to be gradually coming over the American ways of thinking. I tried to compare the "good old times" with the present, very much, of course, to the disadvantage of the latter. The good old times seem everywhere to have been pretty "hard times," but they were such as to create and develope national manhood. This, at any rate, seems to have been the case with the Americans, and now they are enjoying the fruits of their early exertions. As we fly along the Hudson, a beautiful specimen of their country flits past us, with everything that betokens civilization, comfort and wealth; Troy, with its gigantic furnaces, rolling mills and other workshops, and Albany, with the granite walls of the new State-House rising above the highest level of ordinary brick and mortar. Involuntarily, I recall the time when the Dutch at this place ransomed Father Jogues from his Iroquois captors and tormentors. This was over two centuries ago, and Albany was then represented by Fort Orange, "a miserable structure of logs."* Further south there come beautiful cities, like West Point and Newburgh, towns, villages,

* Parkman, Jesuits of North America, p. 229.

farms and villas growing more and more numerous as we approach New York, while, beautifying and mirroring all, there is the noble river, enclosed on the west by the ever varying mountain outline and matchless scenery. Every where there is a teeming, busy population, seemingly enjoying life in the midst of wealth and profusion, so that we are tempted to exclaim of it, "Thou hast eaten, and art "full; thou hast built goodly houses, and hast dwelt therein; "thy herds and thy flocks are multiplied, and all that thou "hast is multiplied." Literally true all this appears to be of the Americans, for nowhere else can such rapid and marvellous material prosperity be witnessed.

A Californian once remarked to me: "There are only "three live cities in the United States, New York, Chicago "and San Francisco." By the adjective "live," he meant venturesome, speculative, extravagant, and may not have been very far wrong. But for solidity and strength, Boston, Philadelphia and St. Louis will probably excel the first named trio. All of them are "live," and, in passing through New York and Philadelphia, the traveller requires to have his wits about him. After a hurried rush through New York, through the business part of Philadelphia, and up to the Centennial buildings, at that time enclosed in mud, I left at midnight on the 21st, by the Pacific express, for San Francisco, there to join a fellow-traveller before proceeding southward. From this on, it was a continual hurry westward, over the Pennsylvania Central, Pittsburgh, Fort Wayne & Chicago, and Rock Island & Pacific railroads to Omaha, which place I reached on the 24th. Notwithstanding the hurry, there is time to obtain glimpses of the Alleghanies, Pittsburg, the Ohio river, Chicago, the Mississippi river, the Prairie country and the Missouri, and some leisure for miscellaneous chatting with

all sorts of people, Canadians included. From the tone of
conversation in the cars, one would suppose that "getting
on in the world" absorbed most intensely the thoughts of
every one. It has been said, I think most unjustly, that
the Americans worship the almighty dollar, but it would
appear to me more correct to say that their idol is material
progress. How this little town is progressing, that one
"played out;" how one man succeeds with his factory, or
somebody else had got "dead broke," forms the subject-
matter of much of the conversation which one hears.
Silent contempt is measured out to places which are going
back, while eager interest is manifested in other localities
which have "taken a start." The city with the greatest
population and the finest streets, the man with the biggest
"pile" and the grandest house, the successful president
of a gigantic railway, the fortunate speculator in a stock or
grain "corner," seem to be objects of huge respect on the
part of the votaries of this modern religion of "getting
ahead." And, indeed, from New York to Omaha there is
food enough for wonder to everyone, though not, perhaps,
for worship. Witness the factories of every description
lining the railways of New Jersey and Pennsylvania; the
shipping and traffic of New York and Philadelphia; the
rolling mills in almost every eastern city; the magnificent
furnaces and Bessemer steel works of Bethlehem and Chicago, the former being the finest establishment of the sort
in the whole world; the coal mines of Pittsburg and Mauch
Chunk; the fertile fields and productive forests of Ohio,
Indiana and Michigan; the vast prairies of Illinois and
Iowa, many of whose farmers gain not only their food from
the soil, but also their fuel from beneath it; the fleets of
steamers and schooners on the great lakes, and lastly, the
iron road across the continent, besides many marvels on its

Pacific slope. To the observant traveller, nothing is better fitted to give him, rapidly, some idea of the power, progress and wealth of the United States, than the ride from New York to San Francisco.

At the same time the conscientious observer must note that there is in the manner and conversation of many of the people much that is far less worthy of his interest and commendation. There is the universal card playing, the frequency of profane language, the prevalence of debasing conversation, the loud talking and forward behaviour of many among the American travelling public. I well remember an instance of extraordinary loudness to which I was witness, while travelling from Buffalo to New York by the Erie railway. On this occasion certain young men and women, well dressed, and seemingly above the working class in station, gave themselves great pains to burlesque certain Sunday school hymns. They actually gathered at one end of a sleeping car and sang a parody on "There is a Happy Land," of which I remember this verse:

> I know a boarding house
> Not far away;
> Where they give ham and eggs
> Three times a day.
> Oh, how the boarders yell,
> When they hear the dinner bell,
> And sniff the glorious smell,
> Three times a day.

This was certainly a very striking proof to me of the want of reverence which is said to characterize the present rising generation of the United States. A similar instance to this came under my notice in 1871, while staying in Salt Lake city. It was Sunday, and I had been invited to dine, by a friend, at quite a respectable club there. After dinner, I was somewhat shocked to hear the conviviality at an adjoining table take the form of psalmsinging, and much more so when the guests around joined vigorously in the chorus of a well-known hymn to the words "Crown Him Lord of all." I do not for a moment wish to maintain that this ribaldry is very common in the United States, but I believe that its occasional breaking out, in this manner, is a proof that the social system is not quite free from disease. Nor would I wish it to be supposed that the Americans are any worse in this respect than other nations. I do not think they are; but we have become accustomed to expect from the United States, as the results of the new political and social principles there prevailing, something better than is to be found in old, worn out and corrupted European communities. Having started with a "clean sheet," unencumbered with old world pauperism, ignorance and crime, we naturally expect from United States institutions much better results than have yet been obtained elsewhere. If we attempt to trace back this levity to its cause, we shall probably find it in the overshadowing attention which is given to mere intellectual instruction, the undue importance with which worldly matters are thereby invested, and the consequent tendency which prevails among all classes to "have a good time," or "take comfort," in unmeaning hilarity or mere bodily indulgence.

At Omaha a great change takes place in the traveller's surroundings. Three different railways converge from the east, at Council Bluffs, bringing together many strange faces and enormous accumulations of baggage. All cross to Omaha on the new iron bridge over the Missouri, a great improvement on the ferryboats, which were in use when I passed the Missouri here in 1871, travelling eastward. In the bustle and excitement of claiming, weighing and checking baggage, the passengers have abundant opportunity of introducing themselves to each other. A young gentleman in a shooting coat and felt hat of the latest styles, and carrying an eyeglass and cane, the latter of which he persisted in holding point upwards, was extremely annoyed at the large amount he had to pay for extra baggage. He confided his troubles to me, and I found him to be an Englishman, but recently landed in New York, and bound for Los Angeles, California. In the sleeping car I found that he and I occupied berths exactly opposite to each other, and so we became companions for the voyage. We took into partnership my next door neighbour, an American from Detroit (who turned out to be very humourous, and a most excellent mimic), and, all the way to San Francisco we mutually contributed to each others enjoyment and enlightenment. We were also joined by an old school Vermonter, who, with his wife, was travelling to San Francisco. He had gone to California in early life, had been all through the troublous times of the Vigilance committee, and become quite wealthy from the great rise in the value of real estate in San Francisco. Yet he was by no means enamoured of living in California, and spent a great deal of his time in his native state, distant 3,400 miles from his place of business!

Early in the afternoon we left Omaha, and were soon speeding across the prairies of Nebraska. These are not quite so tame as the level fields of Illinois, and the valley of the Platte (a slight depression in a vast country) adds additional diversity to the undulating character of the landscape. Next morning, when we reach Sydney, we find the surrounding country to be rolling land, interspersed with rounded bluffs, which latter have sometimes horizontal summits, and are rocky and broken on their sides. Sometimes horizontal strata, of what appears to be limestone, crop out at the ends of the bluffs, while, underneath, a talus has accumulated of loose rock and soil. These features seem to be common to a wide extent of country, for I observed them also on the Kansas Pacific railway in 1871. The landscape is destitute of trees, unless in the neighbourhood of rivers, and, in fact, the river courses can be traced by the trees. Towards Cheyenne, rocky outcrops become less frequent, and the "plains" consist of immense undulations, with empty water-courses here and there among them. The whole of these plains, from Omaha to Cheyenne, are supposed to be underlaid by cretaceous and tertiary rocks, the thickness of which must gradually increase to the westward as the ground ascends. Although imperceptible to the traveller, being distributed over 500 miles of distance, the difference of elevation betwixt Omaha and Cheyenne is, nevertheless, 4,000 feet. The approach to the Rocky Mountains by the Union Pacific railroad is quite disappointing, for little or nothing of picturesque mountain scenery is visible. It cannot be compared to the view obtainable from the Kansas Pacific, and Denver City, Colorado, where the mountains of primary rock rise in serrated ridges to the westward, capped by the snowy summits of Gray's and Pike's Peaks. But there, a Pacific railway is an impossibility, whereas, further to the north, at Cheyenne, it seems as if nature had constructed a prolonged embankment, rising out of the plains and reaching to the crest of the Rocky Mountains, thus enabling the railway to scale them with comparative ease. The underlying horizontal strata, butting against the azoic masses to the westward, seem here to have escaped denuding influences, whereas, in Colorado, these same crystalline masses have been washed completely bare. Granite is intersected near Sherman at an elevation of 8,235 feet, but it is altogether different in character from the greissoid granite of the Colorado mining districts, and is far more prone to disintegrate. At Red Buttes the traveller is awestruck to find, at this great height, unmistakable evidence of the action of the ocean on horizontal strata of sandstones and shales. These rocks have been worn into curiously shaped bluffs, pillars and pinnacles, much resembling those to be seen on a grander scale in Saxon Switzerland. There, the Bastei, the Winterberg, and many other hills and rocks, show similar peculiar forms, and consist of the upper Quadersandstein, which is also a member of the Cretaceous system. The same cretaceous and tertiary rocks are supposed to underlie the Laramie Plains, which stretch away 80 miles to the north-westward, covered with ice-coated snow, and appearing, to the eye of a northerner, like a vast frozen lake. The sun was setting as we left Laramie station to cross them, and I experienced the same desolate, helpless feeling as when leaving port and the ships bows are pointed out towards the pathless ocean.

After leaving Cheyenne, which, with Laramie, is a starting point for the notorious Black Hills country, the conversation turned upon the excitement then prevailing as to gold discoveries there. Advertisements were frequently seen describing in glowing terms their attractions. At the same time rumours were current about starvation and death among the unfortunate people who had been tempted to the district in question. As to gold and minerals, it was asserted by some that nothing of the sort was to be found there. But still false representations continued to be made, and some people were always found to believe them. My English friend was indignant at the deceit thus practiced, and conversation sprang up betwixt him and the Vermonter, who remarked :

"California was settled in the same way."

"How?" enquired the Englishman, with evident surprise.

"The transportation companies, in the early times, circulated exaggerated reports about the abundance of gold in California, and so induced people to emigrate thither. They carried the same specie backwards and forwards in their ships, entering it each time as a new shipment from the Golden State."

"And what became of the emigrants?"

"Those who could, remained and fought it out, but many returned to the east."

Here the Detroiter struck in: "With those who could not it was 'root hog or die!' It's the way to settle a new country!"

"Would it not be better to spend a little more time on the operation and do it honestly?" enquired the Englishman.

"I think not; if there's any good in the country let's have it out; the sooner the better," said the Detroiter.

"But, after all, the country is not yours; the Black Hills are reserved for the Indians. Why does not your government keep out the intruders?"

"They can't do it; and besides, as old Quincy Adams said, we have to 'replenish the earth and subdue it.'"

"But that does not justify you in robbing and exterminating the Indians. 'All men are born free and equal.'"

"That does not apply to Indians. Look at them as you pass the stations. How can they be equal to white men?"

"That *you* ought to be able to say."

"A western man cannot admit the indian as his equal any more than the southerner the negro, or the californian the chinaman."

"Why, chinamen are well-behaved and industrious enough," said the Britisher.

"But a californian will not consider them his equals, and will scarcely regard them as men."

"I understand that. We have all heard of the accident which killed two men *and a Chinaman*. But do you not see that the theory of your constitution, as regards equality, fails, when put into practice? You Americans begin at the wrong end; you propound your theories, and then try to work them out, not being very anxious whether you succeed or no. We English adopt the opposite method, of collecting facts first and theorizing afterwards. We work upon existing practice, and try to improve it, leaving the principle, or theory, to come in afterwards."

Neither the Vermonter nor the Detroiter seemed disposed to follow the Englishman into a discussion on the merits of the inductive method, but I fully agreed with him. I was also forcibly struck with the remark of the Detroiter, that the United States government was powerless to exclude intruders from the Indian country. This was no doubt a fact,* and I could not regard it otherwise than as a proof that the passion of the people for material advancement had been suffered to override every other consideration. It is as if dissoluteness were creeping into the body politic, and incapable of being controlled by any higher principle. This is scarcely to be wondered at, seeing that there is no source for any such higher principle in the American system. If, as President Woolsey of Yale college maintains, the American political system is purely secular, and just as suitable for a nation of Esquimaux or Turks as for the United States, it is hard to see where the controlling higher or religious principle can come in. It is a favorite

* See President Grant's last message.

expression in the States that "religion has nothing to do with politics," which is, alas! but too true in more than one sense. If not only church and state, but religion and the nation, have parted company; if civil government has been divorced from Christianity, it follows that the antidote which the latter has in all ages furnished to national and individual selfishness, cannot be forthcoming to leaven the policy of the United States government.

Sunday morning, the 26th of March, found us at Green river, whose waters, running southward, join the Colorado river, and empty into the gulf of California. Indeed, from Cheyenne to Utah, the railway, for the most part, runs rudely parallel with the line of watershed, whence spring the Missouri, Platte, Colorado and Columbia rivers.

At Green river and the next station, Bryan, the hills around consist of horizontal strata of grey sandstone and shale, which cause the summits to be flat and long drawn. Those flat-topped mountains rise, however, in ranges behind each other, giving quite a peculiar and not uninteresting character to the country, which is preserved until we pass from Wyoming into Utah Territory. Near Piedmont we were delayed two hours by snowdrift, but, as if in compensation, we had an opportunity of observing how a snow plough with three engines behind it handles the snow on these mountains. It frequently forms walls eight or ten feet high on both sides of the track, and more frequently still, it completely covers over the numerous snowsheds. At Evanston, among other things, there are extensive mines of lignite, of great importance in working the railway. In age it no doubt corresponds with the brown coal formation of North Germany, and is probably associated with tertiary rocks. From the coal regions we decend rapidly through the Weber, and Echo cañons to the great Salt Lake Valley, crossing on the way the Azoic rocks of the Wahsatch range. The sides of these cañons are in many places almost perpendicular, and consist of dark red sandstone and shales. The word "cañon" seems to be applied to a depression worn down into these horizontal strata by eroding agents, and having in cross section more or less the shape of the letter U. It is a very different thing from a "gulch," which, as encountered in Colorado, is a V shaped glen, occurring mostly in highly inclined crystalline schists.

While rushing down the cañons, comfortably seated in the cars, viewing what had cost ante-railroad travellers many a toilsome weeks journey to reach, the passengers remarks naturally ran on Utah and its first settlers. Glimpses were often obtained of the old emigrant road along which Mormons and Californians had toiled in early times. I had visited Utah in 1871, and knew something of Salt Lake City and its neighbourhood, and now conversed with the Vermonter as to what must have been the feelings of the Mormons when they day after day plodded wearily over these grey sandy wastes, which we had traversed in twenty-four hours. How their faith must sometimes have been shaken as was that of the Israelites of old, and how they must have exulted on reaching Salt Lake Valley, and finding their promised land. To them it must have appeared that Jehovah himself had guided them to this very spot, for even its physical features resemble those of Palestine. Great Salt Lake plainly corresponds to the Dead Sea, and Utah Lake to the Sea of Galilee. It is easy to see why they called the river connecting them, the Jordan, but, on the other hand, it is perhaps significant, that Salt Lake City occupies rather the position of Sodom than of Jerusalem.

Much of this was discussed by my fellow-travellers, among

whom the Vermonter seemed disposed to agree with some of my observations and opinions. " But after all," said he, " the Mormons suffered and accomplished no more than our " ancestors."

" That's so," said the Detroiter, " the Pilgrim fathers " were good stock, although they are now-a-days regarded " as rather stale heroes."

" May be, but they compare more worthily with the " Iraelites than do the Mormons," said the Vermonter, who had been ruminating on the subjects of our afternoon's conversation.

" Certainly," said the Detroiter, " They came out of the " land of Egypt, out of the house of bondage." " That was " old England, you know," he added, turning to her representative.

" Where they had plenty of beer and roast beef," said the Englishman.

" And where they had cruel taskmasters," said the Vermonter, " and were not allowed to worship the God of their " fathers."

" But how about the Red Sea and the wilderness," asked the Detroiter.

" Well, many of them fought their way through blood, " and sailed over a wilderness of waters."

" Didn't they think of the flesh pots?" asked the Englishman.

" No; they must have been too sea-sick," remarked the Detroiter.

" But they arrived at last, and drove out the Canaanite," said I, and, with the Vermonter, tried to continue the analogy. We talked of the manner in which the first emigrants took possession, meeting with, encroaching on, subjugating and exterminating tribe after tribe of the red men,

3

and of how his lands were divided among the tribes of Europe, just as that of the Canaanites was given to the descendants of the sons of Jacob, for an inheritance. Less homogeneous were, however, the invaders from Europe, who came in and possessed the land of this continent; but the result was the same. Frenchmen in Canada, Puritans in New England, Dutch in New York, Quakers, Swedes and Germans in Pennsylvania, Cavaliers in Virginia, Spaniards and Portuguese in Florida, Mexico and South America, all encountered the Indian and dealt with him in many a different way, with the invariable result of driving him out. Then these tribes increased and multiplied, for they had heard of, and been brought to, a wonderful country; "a "good land; a land of brooks and water, of fountains and "depths, that spring out of valleys and hills; a land of "wheat and barley, and vines and fig trees and pomegran- "ates; a land of oil olive and honey; a land wherein thou "shalt eat bread without scarceness; thou shalt not lack "anything in it; a land whose stones are iron, and out of "whose hills thou mayest dig brass."

"Iron and brass!" broke in the Detroiter. "Those are "base metals; they don't want them in this sweet occident. "Silver and gold is all they care for! Look at Nevada "and California!"

"Look at the Emma mine; there may be silver there, "but there isn't any money," said the Englishman, getting up, yawning, and extinguishing the conversation.

In the evening we arrived at the Mormon town of Ogden, where we had to give up the car and berth we had enjoyed for the three previous days, and transfer ourselves and baggage to the accommodations of the Central Pacific railroad. After an hour's delay we started again, and were soon skimming around the edge of the Great Salt Lake, its heavy waters reflecting the stars of the south. The Englishman was absorbed in a book he had picked up at Ogden station on the Doctrine and Covenants of the Mormons, and at last broke out :

"What fools people must be to believe such rubbish."

"Their practice is better than their doctrine," said the Detroiter.

"How about Polygamy," asked the Englishman.

"That is a mere abuse soon to be remedied; but look at "their thrift and industry."

"They are, indeed, a wonderful people in that respect," said the Englishman.

"Yes," said the Vermonter, "I only wish the descend-"ants of our Puritan forefathers would imitate them."

"How?" asked the Detroiter; "what fault have you to "find with the boys?"

"They seem to think they can retire from business and "live on the reputation of their predecessors."

"I can't see that. I find the boys smart enough."

"Well, I suppose it *is* smartness. I've a nephew in the "east, who had a splendid education, a good example at "home, and $8,000 left him when his father died. Now, "he runs round the country idle, and up to all sorts of mis-"chief, keeps fast horses, and, by way of showing how rich "he is, lights his cigar with a ten dollar bill."

"That's an extreme case," said the Detroiter.

"I'm not so sure about that; and then the new genera-"tion of girls is turning out bad. When I was east last "time, I visited a sister of mine who had grown up daugh-"ters, sixteen and eighteen years of age. They could not "prepare a decent meal of victuals."

"That isn't an indispensable accomplishment," said the Detroiter.

"Isn't it, though?" asked the Vermonter; "it was so considered when I was a young man. I asked my sister, says I, '*was* you brought up in this way? did our parents rear us up so shiftless.'"

"Your sister probably kept the girls at school," said the Detroiter, "girls must have a good education now-a-days."

"Of course," said I, "girls must be educated, but they need not be spoiled; they ought to be kept in training."

"In training!" exclaimed the Englishman, "you wouldn't make them walk an hour before breakfast, and sweat themselves to death, and deny themselves all manner of dainties?"

"Or lift dumbbells and twist indian clubs?" said the Detroiter.

"Training means a great deal more than when applied to athletes and oarsmen, but I would like to see the word restricted in its application, and used to denote the development of the physical powers only."

"But what has bodily development to do with cooking?" asked the Detroiter.

"It is by a certain training of the body," I replied, "guided, of course, by higher qualities, that a good cook is produced."

"Well," said the Detroiter, "I am inclined to agree with you. I never yet came across a good cook who had a large library on the subject. Her art seemed to be seated in her fingerends."

"I have always thought there ought to be special schools for cooking, as well as for other accomplishments," said the Englishman.

"That is surely a mistake; schools seem to be intended for educating the mind only," said I.

"Then where would you have our young people trained?" asked the Vermonter.

"The girls at home; the boys in the workshop," was my prompt answer.

"Then your training means fitting them to earn a 'living.'"

"Pretty much," I replied, and I proceeded to explain my understanding of the matter. I maintained that the thorough developement of the whole individual is the object of true education; that the body and soul, or heart, of man, have an existence as well as the mind, and that to educate the latter only is a mistake fatal alike to the individual and the nation. In the case of woman it results in making her totally unfit, physically, for the duties of wife and mother, besides obliterating the intuitive perception and unfaltering faith which are her most valuable attributes. My remarks regarding the training necessary for a prospective wife and mother, obtained the hearty approval of my American fellow-travellers, and elicited from them a good deal of information regarding the life of American women, which, for several reasons, cannot be reproduced here, but which had the result of deepening my conviction that their training, if not their whole education, is radically defective.

We passed the night of the 26th March oblivious of the peculiarities of the so-called "Great American Desert," through which we were passing. Next morning found us at Wells, Nevada, and speeding over plain after plain, around which are posted picturesque groups of snow-clad mountains, not flattopped or long drawn, but peaked and sawedged, or, like huge waves, foamy and broken-crested. These ranges are not continuous, but in many instances rise out of the level plain, and, at their bases, horizontal terraces are to be seen, indicating the position of ancient beaches. Further west, on the Humboldt river, these picturesque mountains sometimes give place to rounded hills, through the sides of which cliffs project of rudely columnar rock. West of Palisade, rocks with amygdaloidal or cavernous structure seem to occur, but, after all, lithological determinations are unreliable, when the observer is travelling past at the rate of forty miles an hour.

From Palisade a narrow-guage railroad starts southward to the mining regions of Mineral hill and Eureka, which I had also visited in 1871. At that time I had performed the journey of 80 miles on the top of a Concord coach, and have even now a vivid impression of its miseries. At Palisade we were joined by several mining men, and we seemed afterwards to be moving in quite a new atmosphere, mines and mining, "lodes" and "bonanzas," being talked about with great earnestness, for about this time the production of bullion in Nevada had increased enormously, and was, in fact, deranging the specie markets of the world. At Palisade we had seen piles of "base bullion" (ingots of argentiferous lead) awaiting shipment, which had come from the Eureka mining district. Very profitable mines are said to be in operation there, but as regards Mineral Hill, which lies about half-way between Palisade and Eureka, the accounts are not so encouraging. This place was the scene, not long ago, of a mining swindle, by which an old and respectable English firm was sadly victimized. Commenting upon this brought up the inevitable Emma, and the Detroiter said:

"After all, the English cry too much over spilt milk. "Why don't they go to work and make the best of their "mine?"

"Why should they throw good money after bad," said

the Englishman, "and spend more money among the people
" who have cheated them?"

"They were cheated as much in London as in Utah.
" Baron Grant got quite as much money as the American
" proprietors."

"Is Baron Grant one of your English noblemen?" asked
the Vermonter.

"No," replied the Englishman, testily, "he is a pro-
" moter of limited companies, but he is said to have a
" Portuguese title; hence the verse current about him in
" London—

"A King can title give, but honor can't;
" Rank, without honor, is a *barren grant.*
" That's very true, but there's a worse dilemma—
" To be without a title—like the Emma.

"Come now, let's have done with the Emma," said a
gentleman from Eureka. "There are plenty of English
" companies making money in California and Nevada."

"Yes, but it is by hard, close work," said I. "None of
" your magnificent things come into English lands. Witness
" the Comstock mines."

"But look at their misfortunes. In 1868 they were
" regarded as almost valueless, and just as they began to
"flourish again, Virginia city and all their mills and shaft-
"houses were swept away by fire."

"When did that happen?"

"On the 26th October last; and yet, within seven weeks
" afterwards, the engines were rebuilt and at work again."

"There is nothing like American energy; but is it not
" sometimes misapplied in mining?"

"How?" asked my Eureka friend.

"Let me explain; I understand that mining began on
" the Comstock lode, in 1860, and yet some of the shafts
" are down 1700 feet; a depth only reached in European

"mines after centuries of work. In the mines around
" Freiberg, Saxony, for instance, only 600 to 900 feet were
" added to their depth in the course of the century previous
" to 1867."

" Well?"

" Well ; as the Comstock mines are treated, unworkable
" depths will soon be reached ; and what will then become
" of the city and the communities built up around them?"

"That's their look out."

" No! the state is bound to take some care of their
" interests, and those of the public further distant."

" How can that be done?"

"As in Europe ; by prohibiting a rate of production
" beyond the capacity of the mine. I understand that in
" February last the consolidated Virginia product was
" $2,820,000."

"I rather think that month's work was a 'spurt.'"

" So much the worse. But still the year's production is
" not less than twenty millions. How long can any mine
" stand that, on a vein only 700 feet long?"

" Perhaps the Nevada mines will hold out longer than
" you anticipate."

"I wish they may, but nothing can excuse the greed
" which takes twenty millions annually from a property
" which only cost half a million in assessments or calls."

"Why should not the profit be made as rapidly as possi-
"ble?" enquired Eureka. "Why should all that capital be
" allowed to lie dormant in the earth?"

"You might as well ask why a farmer should allow dead
" capital to lie in the fields which he has succeeded in
" getting into good heart."

" The cases are not parallel."

" Indeed they are. The farmer keeps his land in good

"condition, so that he may have a steady remunerative production. The thorough miner takes care of his reserves for the same reason."

"Well, I hope you manage things better in the east."

"Oh, it's just as bad there. Think of the Hecla and Calumet mine on Lake Superior, producing 1,000 tons of Ingot copper *monthly;* and not far from it, Keweenaw Point, is studded with abandoned mines and deserted villages."

"A thousand tons a month!" exclaimed the Vermonter. "What is done with it all?"

"About one-half of the copper production of the United States is exported," said I.

"But there is a high import duty," said he.

"So there is; high enough to be prohibitory, and to keep up the price in the States."

"And what becomes of our exported copper?"

"It goes to England, where it can frequently be purchased for less money than in the States."

"So that we Americans tax ourselves in order to support our copper mines?"

"I believe so; but that is quite consistent with the spirit of your government; and your people seem prepared for almost any sacrifice that will stimulate material development."

I received no reply to this, although I wished to show my American friends that it was possible to push their protective policy to extremes—that there was such a thing as pampering the body politic. Although I feel quite convinced that it is the province of government to watch over and secure the material welfare of the community, yet there is little to be gained from overstimulating it. It is to be remembered that disease may be induced in the physical body by luxury and overfeeding, just as much as by want of proper sustenance; and so it is also with the mining manufactures, trade and commerce of any country. These may be overprotected, so as to become weak and sickly, or so indulged as to become bloated, diseased, and anything but longlived. The enlightened statesman, like the wise parent, or the true physician, must be moderate and careful, and neither allow them to be injured by outside attack, stunted by neglect, or stimulated into excited, unhealthy and merely temporary activity.

After passing Winnemucca, the shades of evening closed in on us, and during the night we passed Reno, where the railway from Virginia city joins the Central Pacific. The morning of the 28th March found us in California, and careering through snow sheds and tunnels under the snowy peaks of the Sierra Nevada. Here and there glimpses are obtained of pine-covered ridges and ravines. At Cape Horn the train stops to admit of the passengers enjoying the splendid view into the Valley below, with the foaming white riverband at the bottom. Then we pass yellowish gray, schistose rocks, standing on edge and much decomposed, and excavations in the alluvium, the traces of former gold hunting. Picturesque cottages are also seen, with gardens containing peach trees in blossom, while not far off patches of snow are sheltered in the nooks around the rocks. Gradually we leave the snow of the Sierra behind us, and soon enjoy genial spring weather, besides the rich, deep green of full-leaved trees, and a good breakfast at Colfax. Soon again we start and hurry through delightful sylvan scenery, broken by granite *in situ* and in large blocks at Rocklin, to a more level but still slightly undulating tract of wide grass and pasture fields, with isolated trees scattered through it. This continues until the dome of the new State-House of California comes into view, and soon we cross the American river and reach Sacramento. The descent from the mountains to this place has been compared with the descent from the Alps into Italy, and, so far as climatic considerations go, no doubt the comparison will hold. The change is simply from winter to summer, and that in the course of a forenoon. But the difference in altitude betwixt the Mont Cenis tunnel and the plains of Lombardy is about 1,500 feet less than the difference in level betwixt Summit Station and Sacramento. While travelling westward for 100 miles betwixt these two points, we descend 7,000 feet. Nevertheless, as we fly along the valley betwixt Sacramento and Stockton, and look eastward, the Sierra does not present a very imposing outline. Its snow-covered ridge rises behind two ranges of dark hills, but shews very few peaks which are at all marked in height or outline. More attractive than the Sierra is the immense expanse of fertile plain which stretches from north to south along its western base.

It is this valley which yields the large grain crop of California, which is increasing year by year, and threatening to overtop in value all the other resources of the state. It is curious, sometimes, to hear discussions going on as to the relative value of its various products. My Eureka friend maintained that the Golden State still deserved its name, as the greatest gold-producing region in the world, while the Vermonter was of opinion that the wheat was more reliable, and brought more real profit to the community. The Detroiter took a middle view, and said:

"Well, I believe fruit-raising to be the most reliable business, although, perhaps, not the most profitable."

"Give us your reasons," said the Englishman, who was going into the business in question at Los Angeles.

"I reason from general principles," said the Detroiter. "The business which ministers to the vices of mankind is always most profitable, while that which provides him with necessities is least so. Betwixt these two extremes lie those occupations which serve to furnish him with luxuries or the more innocent pleasures. These he can't deny himself, and so fruit-raising and kindred businesses must flourish."

"Your philosophy may apply to distilling, tavern-keeping, gambling-houses and brothels, but I cannot see how the precious metals minister to the vices of mankind," said Eureka.

"They are, at any rate, the root of all evil; and as for gold and silver hunting, in its early stages, it is very productive of almost every form of vice."

"Yes," said the Vermonter; "witness San Francisco twenty years ago. But do you really consider wheat-raising unprofitable?"

"Of course it is, in the long run. What I know about farmers is, that they are always dreadfully hard up."

"To me California seems to be troubled with an embarrassment of natural riches," said the Englishman.

"That's so," said Eureka; "but what are these without development? They were in existence all the time the Mexicans held the country. It is not yet thirty years ago since it was ceded to us, and look at what our population and institutions have since made of it."

There was no denying Eureka's facts, but yet I inwardly disliked his language. I had heard much of the same description before from Americans, and at last it dawned upon me that this tone was very much the same as that against which Moses warned the Israelites of old. It was, in fact, as if they had used the words, " My power, "and the might of mine hand, hath gotten me this "wealth."

There are few railway journeys more delightful than that from Sacramento to San Francisco. It winds through the Sacramento, San Joaquin and Alameda valleys, and crosses some of the hills of the coast range, which seem to be built up of sandstones and shales, in a position but little removed from horizontal. We pass immense tracts of green pasture and wheatland, beautiful orchards, charming dwellings, picturesque bluffs, crowned with most luxurious foliage, broad rivers, and frequently the Bay of San Francisco comes into view. The magnificent scenery almost excites the mind, and simultaneously impresses it with the idea that here, if anywhere in the western hemisphere, is to be found the land "flowing with milk and honey." It is, besides, studded with flourishing towns, such as Stockton, Ellis and Oakland—the latter being the Brooklyn of San Francisco, although distant from it five miles—across the bay. At Oakland the Englishman was picked up by a friend from Los Angeles, and bade us, heartily, good bye! Viewed from Oakland, San Francisco does not appear very imposing to the traveller from the east, owing to the distance; and, after getting on board the steam ferry, his attention is absorbed by other matters, and he is apt to omit obtaining a nearer view of this really magnificent city from the bay. I had to take leave of my other travelling companions, whose destinations in San Francisco were all different from mine, and I believe we all very sincerely expressed the great pleasure we had had in each other's company. I soon afterwards landed, and found my way to the Palace Hotel, a splendid structure, and really worthy of its rather magniloquent name. It ought, however, to be mentioned, that it is named after the Palais Royal, in Paris, and that its distinguishing feature is the beautiful courtyard, with its central fountain and the carriageway round it; the whole completely roofed in with glass.

I had only one clear day, the 29th March, in which to attend to business and see a little of San Francisco. Here I was joined by the gentleman who was to accompany me on the Pacific trip. He was a resident of San Francisco, but understood Spanish thoroughly. In this narrative he will go by the name of Armstrong. After our arrangements had been made for sailing next day, I found I had a few hours to spare for a stroll through the city. There are several points in its northern part from which its surroundings of mountains and valleys, bay and ocean can be viewed. These are simply of indescribable variety and beauty. As to the city itself, the wharves, churches and hotels are the most conspicuous objects. The public buildings are less prominent, but some magnificent private residences are to be seen. In some instances a whole block is occupied with the buildings and dependencies used for the accommodation of one family only. Surely this is "building goodly houses and dwelling therein." Although San Francisco is far from being so lawless and licentious as it was in the old time preceding the Vigilance Committee, still it cannot be considered a very moral place. Riches and idleness seem to be producing here their natural fruits in the shape of luxury, extravagance, pleasure-seeking and social corruption. " Satan finds some mischief still for "idle hands to do." I stumbled across a Montrealer in the vicinity of one of the hotels, who, in subsequent conversation had occasion to remark, pointing to the enormous building, "Do you see that hotel? I doubt whether there "is one virtuous woman in it." Among the masculine gender a species of depravity has sprung up sufficiently marked to have originated a new name. "Hoodlum" is a term peculiar to San Francisco, and almost equivalent to "rowdy" in the east. The city is infested with a crowd of young rascals, from sixteen to twenty years of age, to whom this name is applied. They abuse Chinamen, insult Germans, drink, swear, fight, cheat and steal, and it is a problem how the community manages to produce them. They are said to be mostly of Irish origin, and whether this phenomenon is a consequence of Chinese immigration is a question well worthy of discussion. People speak of dull times even in California, the loudest and bitterest complaints coming from the labouring population. The best positions and employments are said to be occupied by the sons of the rich classes, and every branch of labour is monopolized by the Chinese, with whom the white man scorns to compete. There are loud cries in favour of interference on the part of the Federal government to prevent Asiatic immigration, and every white workman who can raise the money goes eastward or back to Europe, cursing the Golden State. To me it seems, however, that the Chinese have only stepped in and occupied vacancies previously existing in the American social system, which have been caused by the false training of their children by American parents. It is well known that, in the Eastern States, native-born girls do not take willingly to domestic service; that those who work prefer to do so in factories and salesrooms. This always appeared very strange to me, for, in Scotland, domestic servants are usually supposed to rank a little higher, socially, than girls working in mills and bleachworks. Still, it is unquestionable, that among the Americans the idea prevails that disgrace attaches to kitchen or laundry work, and consequently it is done by Irish and German girls in the east, and by Chinamen in the west. Then, on the other hand, there is no system of apprenticeship in the United States, and a decided preference on the part of the boys for gentlemanly occupations, whereat they will not be obliged to soil their hands. The parents seem to yield, and to be blind to the fact that their weakness produces " loafers " in the east and "hoodlums" in the west.

It is, indeed, strange, that under a government which makes such extraordinary exertions for the sustenance and proper development of trade and manufactures, the training of the bodies of the young people, by work in kitchen, field and factory, to thorough efficiency in practical occupations, is so much neglected. Stranger still, the whole matter appears, when it is taken into consideration that the *home* is really the object of the American's chief solicitude. In warding off attacks from without on the industries of his country, he does not seek merely to accumulate wealth for himself. He is not ungenerous, and no one is more ready to give any one "a show " and a helping hand who exerts himself with a will to improve his position. The American wishes to provide himself with a comfortable, and even luxurious home, and he does not grudge the workman his high wages, but delights to see his neighbors, of every description, enjoying comfort and decency. But, heretofore he has merely looked at the material aspect of things; he has been absorbed by the consideration that bread and butter are essential to the production of a happy home. He has also, it must be confessed, made ample provision for the mental education of the rising generation. But he has yet to learn that there are other things, besides, essential to the creation of a happy, contented and prosperous domestic circle—namely, a training of the body to efficiency, industry and thrift—and such an edification of the heart as will obliterate selfishness and scepticism, and develope the higher life of conscientiousness, charity and faith.

San Francisco is one of the cities in the United States which has banished the Bible from its schools, and California has taken the lead in suppressing prayer to the Almighty within its legislative halls. These circumstances may be regarded as trifles, but even in this case they are the straws which indicate the existence of strong currents of irreligion and infidelity. Thes are the fit accompaniments of that state of mind which exalts the doings of individuals, associations and institutions, and ascribes to them the enormous strides that have been made in the development of the country, and entirely ignores its natural resources. Moses' commands and threatenings to the Israelites would seem fitting and opportune to the inhabitants of California, and, indeed, of a good many other countries. Let us here quote and take them to heart, reverently remembering the everlasting truths which they embody:—"But thou shalt remember the Lord thy God: "for it is He that giveth thee power to get wealth." "And " it shall be if thou do at all forget the Lord thy God, and " walk after other gods, and serve them and worship them, "I testify against you this day, that ye shall surely perish. "As the nations which the Lord destroyeth before your "face, so shall ye perish; because ye would not be obe- "dient to the voice of the Lord your God." (Deuteronomy viii; 18-20.)

II.—THE PACIFIC COAST.

"Like as the arrows in the land of the giant; so are the young children." Psalm cxxvii; 5.

A stiff breeze was blowing from the northwest on the 30th March, 1876, as the Pacific Mail steamer "Montana" left San Francisco and passed through the Golden Gate. The weather was clear, and the passengers promenaded the deck and watched the beautiful shores of the bay and inlet as they glided past. The ship put well out to sea before turning southward, and, although a side-wheel steamer, pitched about a good deal, causing a mysterious disappearance of the passengers. Towards evening I myself found the Pacific Ocean much too unquiet for me, and had to turn in at last, not for the night, but for a couple of days, during which I had time to reflect on the infirmity of human purpose. Many a time and oft had I resolved, when in exactly the same circumstances in former periods of my life, never again to be found at sea; and yet, here was I again, suffering in mind from general demoralization, and in body from violent seasickness. I was utterly disgusted with myself and all the world. Armstrong paid me occasional visits and expressed sympathy, but, of course, he was laughing in his sleeve at my collapse. He tried to get me up, but unsuccessfully. Having sustained the loss of my reputation as a sailor, I thought I might as well secure whatever profit was derivable from retaining a horizonital position.

On the morning of the 2nd April the breeze and swell died away. Armstrong now made another attempt to rouse me, and succeeded, by telling me that land was in sight. So it was, in the shape of a hazy band to the eastward, but it was too far off to be entertaining. It was otherwise with the passengers who, like myself, had found their sealegs. They were very interesting, although of a mixed description, English, French, German and Spanish being freely spoken. There were old Californians on their way to Europe or the Centennial; American Spaniards bound for various Pacific ports; San Francisco Scotchmen and Germans going down to Costa Rica; a couple of Northern men from Ontario visiting Lower California and Guatemala in search of health; a Bostonian on the way back from Australia; a German returning from Japan, etc. A Yankee, from Astoria, Oregon, was very anxious to hear something about the Canadian Pacific railway, and seemed quite overjoyed when I expressed the opinion that it would ultimately be "put through." The fair sex was also well represented, and it became evident to me that I had suffered nothing from the recent epidemic compared to them. They appeared completely worn out, fragile as flowers, but fascinating still to the human insects buzzing around them.

Armstrong, being aware of my efforts to learn Spanish, introduced me to Señor Rafael Asturias, of San Jose, Guatemala, who was on his way back from San Francisco with some fine horses he had bought there. Then followed an expedition forward to the lower deck to see said horses, and a curious conversation betwixt the señor and myself, which I can only compare to the working together of two imperfect gear-wheels with plenty of their teeth broken out. We succeeded best in our efforts at mutual understanding when seated on the upper deck aft, with grammar and dictionary before us. I studied very assiduously for a couple of days, until I was complimented by the ladies for my diligence and my modest, retiring behaviour. Among them were the daughters of the Oregonian and a Mrs. Krumbach, a German lady from San Francisco, and I was forced to excuse myself and ascribe my seeming bashfulness to the extreme respect and reverence which I entertained for the fair sex. I quoted, in self-justification, to Frau Krumbach, certain lines from Goethe's Torquato Tasso, of which I was at once ordered to furnish a translation for the benefit of the other ladies. I here transcribe it :

> Becomingness surrounds as with a wall
> The tender, fragile, easily-injured sex ;
> Where decency prevails, there do they rule,
> Where boldness tyrannizes, they are nought.
> And do we ask both sexes what they crave—
> Man freedom wants ; Woman propriety.

I doubt, however, whether the quotation was appreciated, for the safeguard in question is seldom provided for American ladies ; and its value is very much underrated by the average American masculine mind. Had this been otherwise we would, in all probability, never have heard of the scandals which for such a long time agitated the New York world. That which is proper, fitting or becoming in behaviour or manner, is not much studied by American mothers, and they are not apt to follow European customs in the matter. Here the discipline of the heart and morals is defective, and the movements of the young people not sufficiently controlled. This is not an affair of mental or religious instruction to be attended to in week-day or Sunday school, but mostly demands training under the parents eye at home.

During this time the "Montana" was leaving behind her about 240 miles a day of the 3,330 miles distance from San Francisco to Panama. The temperature had risen gradually from 55°. at San Francisco to 73° off the coast of Lower California. On the 4th we approached quite close to the latter, for the steamer has to touch at Cape St. Lucas. The outlines of the mountains on the shore and behind it were very rugged and picturesque, and I perceived two peaks inland resembling in form the paps of Jura. The sight of the land, the warm air and the calm sea, brought all the passengers on deck, who really seemed to enjoy the scenery presented by the coast as it glided past during the sunny afternoon. We were all beginning to enjoy the excellent fare provided on board the steamer, and at the sound of the dinner bell found our way down stairs very promptly. The newest feature—or rather features—at our meals, were those of the Chinamen, and neither Irish nor negro waiters could possibly exceed them in alacrity and desire to please. They wore their native dress and pigtail, and although they were quite numerous, the passengers had only one name for them. "John!" "John!" was the cry on all sides; while they replied, "Yes, sull; hele, sull; lice and cully, sull; all light." Why they persisted in substituting the letter l for r I never found out. John's English is very peculiar, and he occasionally incorporates with it Spanish words. He has, for instance, appropriated the Spanish verb *saber*—to know. "Me no sabe," is his way of expressing "I don't know." Speaking Spanish correctly he ought to say, "Yo no se;" but John is not very particular. After dinner every one hurried on deck to see Cape St. Lucas, the most southern extremity of Lower California, which we passed about nine P. M. Huge rocks jut out into the sea, and many rocky islands rise out of it off the Cape. A bonfire was lit on one of the eminences a short distance from the shore, showing that the approach of the steamer had been noticed. A boat put off, delivered and received letters, and then the steamer's bows were turned southeastward on its smooth and starlit course across the Gulf of California.

The morning of the 5th found the ocean still placid as a lake, although in crossing the entrance of the gulf a rougher sea is frequently experienced. The passengers moved about quietly and smoothly, for nothing was visible on the wide, calm waters to attract their attention or elicit their remarks. The temperature was that of a model summer morning, and man and nature seemed to be aware that it was Sunday. A slight stir was noticed as the passengers read the announcement regarding service. At 11 A. M. the captain takes his place in the midst of a small congregation, among whom the most earnest worshippers appear to be the steerage passengers. Chant, prayer and hymn follow each other in wonted order, all carefully and devoutly conducted, and with the prayer for blessing, "where two or three are gathered together," the service ends. But it is safe to say that not one-fourth of the cabin passengers attended it. The Oregonian was absent, although his two daughters had conducted the musical part of the service. I joined him afterwards and expressed my regret at his absence.

"Well, you see, my daughters attended the Church "academy at home, which is a good school and well-looked "after by the Bishop; but I, myself, am not much of a "churchgoer."

"I'm sorry at that."

"Well, religious affairs are not of much account. I "find just as trustworthy people outside as inside of the "churches."

"Perhaps so; but it may be that these same people owe "their trustworthiness to early religious education."

"I have no reason for thinking so; in fact, our American

"system of education, which is second to none in the world, takes no account of religion at all."

"But the people you speak of may have been educated before the American system came into existence."

"I never thought of that."

"Now, I've had Germans working for me who had thrown away all the religious doctrine they had been taught in their youth, but still they were conscientious, upright men, because the effect of early religious discipline can never be wholly obliterated."

"But you don't mean to say that in Germany the young are taught religion?"

"Certainly I do."

"Why, our system, which is quite secular, is founded upon that of Prussia."

"That is to say, you have adopted the tragedy of Hamlet, and left out Hamlet's part."

"I don't understand."

"Why, the Prussian system is essentially a religious one. In fact, dogmatical religion is taught as regularly in the Prussian schools as arithmetic."

"Well, now you're going too far."

"I refer to Schlesinger here," said I, appealing to a San Francisco German with a very Jewish cast of features.

"You are right," said he; "it's so; but the nonsense they teach, under the name of religion, makes as many unbelievers as the unsectarian system."

"Pardon me," said another German—whose name, being translated, was Cook—"you are too one-sided; our poet, Uhland, says—

    "For faithfulness the German people's famed;
    That have I heard, and that I firm believe."[*]

---

[*] Ernst von Schwaben.

"And further, I believe that its faithfulness, truth, honesty and humbleness is attributable to its religious system of education."

"And further I believe," said I, "that if the state undertakes the education of the subject, it ought to do so thoroughly, and develope the whole man, body, mind and soul."

"I hate to hear people talk about a soul," said Schlesinger. "I believe in a mind, but not in a soul. Prove to me that I've a soul, and then I'll believe it."

"Prove to me that you have a mind, and then I'll believe it," I retorted.

Schlesinger was ready to reply, but Cook took my arm for a promenade and afterwards remarked: "You may be able to do some good in candidly discussing these matters with one individual, but not when three or four mix themselves up in the conversation."

On the morning of the 6th April we sighted the Mexican coast, and the mountains of the Province of Guerrero, which rise in serrated ridges one behind the other far back into the country, the outline of the most distant melting into the clouds. The whole day was passed sailing along the coast, always in view of the most picturesque landscapes, which fully absorbed the attention of the passengers.

"What a splendid country it is to be sure! that Mexico," said the Oregonian to me.

"Indeed it is; what a pity it should be held by such a miserable people," said I.

"The people are bad, but the priests are worse."

"The Devil is not so black as he's painted. They may yet waken up to see the necessity of leading the people onward, instead of keeping them back."

"You might as well expect to see water flow up hill."

"Still, you will admit that it would be a good and right thing if they could be got to serve the state faithfully, and consent to train up the young in learning and true piety."

"I don't see that it can be any of their business. Priests or parsons should never be allowed to meddle with education in a really free country."

"I, on the contrary, believe that it is absolutely essential to the well-being of the state that it should insist upon religious education."

"You surprise me! Why is the state bound to take up such a position?"

"Please answer me a few questions first. Is it not essential to the well-being of society that justice should be well and faithfully administered?"

"Yes."

"Is not the state charged with such administration?"

"Yes."

"Is it not essential to the proper administration of justice that every means should be used for obtaining reliable evidence?"

"Yes."

"Is reliable evidence obtainable from a witness who is not impressed with the sanctity of an oath, and does not understand its nature?"

"I suppose not, but—"

"Excuse me! In order that a witness may rightly regard his oath, should he not be taught to believe in the existence of the Deity, and in the doctrines of a future state, and of future rewards and punishments?"

"Well, perhaps so; but I believe that the oath should be abolished; it does not signify much now-a-days, and a great many of our lawyers think that it might be entirely dispensed with."

"Why, you almost take away my breath! abolish the oath! That is the best proof that your secular system is making it less and less effectual. It renders the oath hollow and profitless, and instead of reforming your system you abolish an institution which has been for ages the safeguard of justice. That is a cheap remedy for false swearing, but a nasty one. It is as if a doctor were to propose to cure a patient by killing him."

I did not continue the conversation. The Oregonian had wriggled off the hook.

During the whole of the next day a continuation of the same beautiful scenery was exhibited by the coast. In fact it was equivalent to a panorama, and one could have almost fancied that the coast was moving and the steamer lying at rest on the motionless ocean. It became monotonous at last, and card-playing was started here and there. Armstrong and others devoted themselves to the young ladies, who insisted on having poetry written in their scrap-books. I furnished Armstrong with an old effusion of mine for this purpose, which he wickedly led them to suppose had been written for the occasion. Here it is:

WOMAN' EYE.

What orb so brightly gleaming,
With magic witch'ry teeming,
Of mischief slyly dreaming,
    So bold, and yet so shy;
So proud and yet so pleasing,
So fiery, yet so freezing,
So radiant, yet so teasing,
    As woman' laughing eye.

Or what so overjoying,
So care and woe destroying,
Life's bitter cup alloying,
    As woman' first love sigh.
How powerfully prevailing,
How rapt'rously regaling,
The blissful glow exhaling
    From woman' love-lit eye.

> Or, when by ties endearing
> Our lives and lots they're cheering,
> There seems almost appearing
>   A heaven beneath the sky.
> The glorious sun declining,
> To leave us half repining,
> Can ne'er eclipse the shining
>   Of woman's constant eye.
>
> And when thro' ceaseless toiling,
> Encouraged by her smiling
> And innocent beguiling
>   We come at last to die;
> How doubt and death deriding,
> In future bliss confiding,
> Our fears so softly chiding
>   Is woman's hopeful eye

Late in the afternoon the "Montana" steamed into the harbour of Acapulco. It is completely land-locked, on the west by islands and a peninsula, on the east and northeast by the mountainous mainland, through the lowest pass in which a road is seen leading to the City of Mexico. The old Spanish fort, east of the town, is one of the most prominent objects, and the cathedral is another. But the most striking feature of all to a northern eye is the vegetation, and notably the groups of cocoanut palms that border the beach, and the banana, orange and mango trees interspersed among the houses of the city. The latter are built of huge, unburnt bricks, forming walls of enormous thickness (in which I looked in vain for a pane of windowglass), supporting roofs covered with well-burnt tiles. It was towards evening when we visited the town, and found the inhabitants lying around in the hot, dusty streets. A few of them were selling cocoa nuts in the market place, and some mules were being unloaded, but there was no other sign of industry. Some of them were wooly-headed negroes, and the so-called "greasers"—half Indian, half Spanish—were almost indistinguishable from the negroes in colour, but could be detected by their straight black hair. After dark the people seemed to be assembled *en masse* in the market place or *plaza*, where they were treated to an exhibition of fire-works in commemoration of one of their church festivals. I was told that displays of fire-works are indispensable to the celebration of saints' days in Mexico and Central America. "The nearer the church, the further from grace," certainly applies to the inhabitants of Acapulco, for it was here that the populace had murdered a resident Protestant clergyman and some of his converts a few months previously. Some action was taken by the United States government, but no real satisfaction obtained for the outrage, which may be another proof that its politics are innocent of religion. But, indeed, the only way of obtaining satisfaction is to subjugate the whole country, a consummation which all reasonable people desire. Energetic Americans would, at any rate, be much better employed in doing this than in hunting poor Indians in the Black Hills country. A remark to this effect brought out the Bostonian, who asked—

"Why should the Americans take the job in hand?"

"Because they will not allow any one else to interfere, "adopting a sort of dog in the manger policy. France had "to give it up, and as for England, she has no diplomatic "relations with Mexico."

"Uncle Sam will probably move when he gets ready," said the Bostonian. Whereupon I retorted—

"His family are ready enough to preach manifest destiny "in the North, but not to practice it down here."

"Other nations take their own time, and why not the "United States?"

"Why, look at England, how she has conquered and "civilized India, ruling it firmly, but justly."

"Well; why does she not take Turkey in hand as well. "There you have a specimen of 'dog in the manger' policy. "She will neither interfere herself nor allow Russia to do "so. Nay, she has even spilt her best blood for Turkey; "but you cannot say that we ever fought for Mexico."

This view of the case rather upset my argument, and we wound up the debate agreeing that the Spaniards were the Turks of the New World, foreign to its soil and civilization. Like Mr. Gladstone and Mr. Carlyle, we voted that they were nuisances to be ejected at the earliest possible moment, but no resolution was arrived at as to who was to act as policeman.

Next day, the 7th April, we were crossing the Gulf of Tehuantepec, out of sight of land; I therefore devoted an extra hour to the study of Spanish. While so occupied, Señor Asturias was my patient, never-failing companion and instructor, and, by way of compensation, I attached myself to him regularly when he visited his horses forward among the deck passengers. Here I found it quite profitable to chat with old Californian explorers and miners, and with an old Irish couple who were on a pilgrimage to the "ould sod." I had also some interesting talk with a Norwegian lady in her own language. Her husband had died in San Francisco, and she was on her way back to Christiania with her children. I expressed my surprise at her travelling eastward. "The people of your country are "mostly found travelling in the opposite direction. Can "you do as well in Christiania as in San Francisco?"

"Oh, no; I shall soon return there, for my business of "dressmaking pays well, but I shall leave my children with "my relations to be educated."

"What! are there not schools enough in San Fran- "cisco?"

"O, yes, indeed, plenty; but still the children do not turn out well, and have no catechisms, and learn nothing about religion."

"Then, you want them to be reared as you were yourself?"

"Yes; in good, religious Lutheran schools, and afterwards to be examined and cared for by the pastor, and confirmed by the bishop."

"There are plenty of ministers and bishops in San Francisco."

"That may be, but there are too many bad influences, and I don't like the schools; they don't even allow the bible inside of them."

In the afternoon I brought up this new contribution to the consideration of the education question, in conversation with Cook and a few others, and told them of the Norwegian widows experience and opinions.

"I don't wonder at it," said Cook; "if my circumstances would permit it, I would take my children home to Germany for the same reasons."

"Oh! pshaw!" broke in Armstrong; "there is far too much fuss about education. I am a Democrat and a Freetrader, and believe in free trade in schools as well. Let the government and municipalities leave the whole matter to private enterprise."

"And what would then become of the poor man's children?" asked Cook.

"What became of them in by-gone ages? How were Abraham, Isaac and Jacob educated? Where did Robert Burns or George Stephenson or Cornelius Vanderbilt graduate?"

"Oh, come now," said the Bostonian; "that won't do for our day; those were men of genius."

"Exactly so," said Armstrong, "and now we have no "men of that stamp. I'll tell you why: You put all your "boys and girls through the same groove in your educating "machine, and they all come out pretty much of the same "shape, and with every particle of originality squeezed out "of them."

"But surely you would not abolish schools altogether," I asked.

"Yes, I would," replied Armstrong; "all of them, except "those which are self-supporting. This national and gene-"ral education is a delusion and a snare. Now, I ask you, "sir," said he, turning to the Bostonian, "does it not unfit "many for humble but useful positions?"

"Well, of course, it engenders ambition, and, among "poor people, a desire to better their circumstances."

"But does it not unfit them for work? Does it not foster "within them the notion that disgrace is attached to manual "labour?"

"Well, I daresay some such feeling is sometimes pro-"duced, but that must be the fault of the teachers or the "system. True education ought not to produce any such "result."

"I fear," said I, "you are both blaming the schools and "teachers for an effect of which they are not the cause. "If a disinclination for work shows itself, that ought to be "corrected by the parents, not by the teachers."

"But the parents will not take that trouble," said Armstrong, "and the consequence is that the children grow "up to be dolls instead of housewives, and 'hoodlums' "instead of good citizens."

"It is the *duty*," I answered, "of the parents to train "them up properly."

"Just so," said he, "but if American mothers are averse

"even to giving birth to children, they are not likely to be anxious about the best method of training them."

"It ought to be the greatest pleasure in the world to them if they have any faith in Scripture. 'Lo, children are an heritage of the Lord; and the fruit of the womb is His reward.'"

"Armstrong is too severe," said Cook; "American mothers are not so indifferent; their chief fault is that they love their children 'not wisely, but too well,' indulging them too much."

"Yes, that is the case too," admitted Armstrong; "each of them believes that *her* children are of extra superfine quality, and intended only to become ladies and gentlemen."

"Well, well," said Cook, "I don't believe they are exclusively to blame; a great deal depends upon the schools. In Prussia and other German States national education is established of such a description as to produce thrifty and industrious citizens, who are not averse to any description of labour provided it is honest."

"And what," asked I, "is the element in the German system which makes them content to learn and labour truly to get 'their own living, and to do their duty in that 'state of life unto which it has pleased God to call 'them?'"

"I believe it to be diligent instruction in vital, not dogmatical religion."

Here the discussion began to get dry, the interest in it gradually abated, and was at last extinguished by the sound of the lunch bell.

The next day we were still out of sight of land, and obliged to depend for intellectual occupation on our immediate surroundings. Every part of the ship was explored, and I began to observe a little about its internal economy. The temperature was now 85°, but even in the steerage, or lower deck, every place was roomy, airy and clean. The greatest order and most scrupulous cleanliness prevailed. There was none of that close, sickening smell perceivable, which haunts and infects Atlantic ships, and which sticks to their passengers and baggage long after they have landed. The deck hands were all Chinamen, but I doubt whether they would be of the slightest use in a storm on the Atlantic, and perhaps even on the Pacific they may be found unreliable at a critical moment. But Captain Searle, of the "Montana," was a strict disciplinarian, and if constant drill is calculated to improve the Chinamen, they had enough of it. Yet the captain, who was an Englishman, evidently believed in "fair play," would allow no ill usage of the Chinamen, and severely censured the head steward for something of this sort. Every forenoon at 11 o'clock, the captain, followed by the steward or first officer, made a tour of inspection through every part of the ship, looking sharply after everything likely to interfere with the cleanliness of the rooms or comfort of the passengers.

At nine o'clock on the morning of the 10th April we reached San Jose de Guatemala, where Mr. Cook and Señor Asturias left us. The Señor wore a very grave face as he bade us good bye, for war had broken out betwixt Guatemala and Salvador, and prospects occurred to him of billetings and forced contributions. The merits of the quarrel were very obscure to outsiders, but the war seemed to have been precipitated by the Salvador government, which was having the worst of the fighting. Judging from the specimens of soldiers to be seen at San Jose, the "armies" would seem to consist of the merest rabble, and the war to be not much above the level of a faction fight.

In some way or other Honduras is also mixed up in the quarrel, so that the "war" bears some analogy to the celebrated triangular duel invented by Captain Maryatt.

We lay at anchor off San Jose until the evening, taking on board coffee and other freight. There is no harbour here but a long wharf jutting out into the ocean, at which barges are loaded and unloaded, while they heave up and down on the heavy swell rolling in from the west, which breaks with a great roar along the dark brown shingle. The shore is bounded by a dense bank of dark green forest, beyond which no objects of prominence in the interior are seen, although the volcanoes of Old Guatemala, exceeding 14,000 feet in height, cannot be far distant.

Next day we were again out of sight of land, and again obliged to provide ourselves with entertainment out of the limited sphere enclosed by the ship's timbers. Luckily we had had at San Jose an accession of passengers in the persons of three Germans who had been travelling and trading in the interior. They quickly assimilated with Herr Hermann, the passenger from Japan, and formed quite a jolly company. The musical department of the steamer, which had previously been comparatively inactive, now became very animated, and the saloon resounded with the strains of many a chorus and *burschenlied*. The best was "*Mein Lebenslauf ist Lieb und Lust*," which, rendered into English, became a great favorite with the passengers. It ran as follows:

>Our course in life is full of fun,
> And free from care and strife;
>A merry song from healthy lungs
> Cheers up our path through life.
>To-day our way is short and bright,
> To-morrow dark and long;
>But care can only make it worse—
> Not so a merry song.
>   Hurrah! Hurrah!
> Not so a merry song.

> The times are hard, and sorrows grim
> O'er all our spirits brood,
> But where a joyous heart does beat
> The times are choice and good.
> Come, Mirth ! thou welcomest of guests,
> Come dine with us to-day;
> Make humble fare taste sweet to us,
> And sorrows fly away.
>   Hurrah ! Hurrah !
> And sorrows fly away.

On the afternoon of the 12th April we arrived at Punta Arenas (Sandy Point), in Costa Rica. This is another Central American coffee port, at the head of the Gulf of Nicoya, well sheltered and surrounded by very imposing mountain scenery, especially towards the northeast, where the backbone of the country rises to a height of about 10,000 feet. It is quite volcanic in places, and the mountain Irasu is pointed out as being still active. This volcano is said to be quite accessible, and to afford a view of both oceans from the same spot. Here, again, the government is as eruptive as the mountains. There was war between the republics of Costa Rica and Nicaragua about a question of boundary; but, indeed, a state of siege is chronic in Central America. A Spanish gentleman and his family, who had come on board at San Jose, landed here. It turned out that he was an exile from Costa Rica, and could not land without the permission of the president of that republic. This he succeeded in obtaining by telegraph. A great many thought he was a fool for his pains, and that the only place for decent people along this coast was on board the Pacific Mail Company's steamers, which, indeed, become the ultimate refuge of many "patriots."

As a specimen of Central American rule, a few particulars may be given regarding this government of Costa Rica. It borrowed money in England to build a railway across the country. It spent the money, left the railway unfinished, will allow no one to complete it, and leaves its English creditors to mourn the loss of both capital and interest. Meanwhile it carries on an establishment for making fire-works, keeps a rum distillery at work, grows tobacco, and reserves a monopoly of the trade in these articles, which is the principal source of its revenue. The fire-works department is peculiar, but these it seems are indispensable in sustaining the state church. Without them no saint's day could be properly celebrated. Yet the "Liberals" are in power in Costa Rica, and the Jesuits have been expelled. From what I heard, however, they are not the only people who bring disgrace upon the church. Many of the clergy lead openly immoral lives, and are not ashamed to acknowledge their illegitimate offspring. This reminds one of the days of Henri Quatre, when Madame D'Estree, the sister of the King's mistress, and an Abbess, reared up her daughters in her own convent. The lower classes are said to be much neglected by the clergy, and many couples live in a state of concubinage because of their inability to pay the fees to the church for getting married. It does not, therefore, seem that the Jesuits, or the existence of a despotic government, could make this state of things any worse.

We left Punta Arenas during the night, and next morning found ourselves sailing along a picturesque coast. But we had also something in the ocean to attract our attention, in the shape of whales, sharks, porpoises and turtles. The latter were to be seen in great numbers, almost motionless, raising their heads languidly to look at the steamer as it passed, and slowly moving their ungainly paws. Those were objects of great interest to the lady passengers, to whose service Armstrong and others had long since devoted themselves exclusively. They were evidently becoming very much interested in them just as the voyage was about to terminate. So much was this the case that I found poor Armstrong puzzling his matter of fact head in an attempt to string together some rhyme at the command of a fair Oregonian. I tried to help him, with the following result:

THE TURTLE TO THE TURTLEDOVE.

Said the turtle in the water
 To the turtle-dove on deck—
Why gazest thou upon me
 With elongated neck?

Dost thou design to hook me,
 Or catch me in thy net,
And into soup to cook me,
 Real turtle soup, you bet!

Go on! careering steamboat;
 And you, proud Miss—depart!
Real turtle soup shall never
 Delight your weary heart.

Seek thou a city lover,
 Adorned with a calf's head,
And out of that prepare you
 Mock-turtle soup instead.

For me! in this salt ocean,
 With heavy fin I'll ply
My leisurely vocation,
 Live well—and freely die.

But weightier matters than these very often engaged our attention. After Cook landed at San Jose, the Bostonian and I only were left to resist the combined atheistic attacks of Schlesinger and Hermann, supported by the Oregonian and the German legion from Guatemala. Hermann gradually came to the front, overshadowing Schlesinger, whose coarse materialism he disliked. Remembering Cook's counsel, I frequently engaged Hermann, alone, in conversation on the subject, but found him very difficult to impress with other than the most tangible considerations. As for the Oregonian, he tried to convert me to spiritualism, and it turned out that he, who was ready to criticise and reject all evidence and argument from Scripture, was prepared to accept as Gospel the flimsiest rhodomontade contained in newspapers "devoted to the interests of spiritualism."

When I awoke on the morning of the 15th, unwonted stillness reigned, and, on getting on deck, I found the Montana at anchor in the Gulf of Panama, about two miles from the city. The latter is beautifully situated at the foot of a bold, rocky hill, and, as usual, the cathedral is the most prominent building. Cocoa, banana, orange, plantain and other trees are scattered through and around the city, and cover the hills to the northward. On the south the bay is enclosed by half a dozen most picturesque islands, and on the west by a mountainous back ground, while to the southeastward stretches away a long, low, hazy line of coast, beyond which, three centuries and a half ago, Pizarro must have gazed wistfully on hearing the indefinite accounts of the golden country of the Incas. Altogether the scene is very lovely, and reminds one of the subjects of many a very romantic theatrical drop-scene. Indeed, a little smoke rising out of one of the eminences in the east, is all that is wanted to furnish a landscape worthily rivalling the Bay of Naples.

But soon came the bustle of getting our things together, filing on to the tender, and seeing our acquaintances, of sixteen days standing, safely on board the train for Aspinwall. Then came waiting for the baggage; strolling into the town under a vertical sun, our umbrellas shading our feet as well as our faces; trading with the natives in oranges and pine apples; and hunting up stragglers. Then the cry came, "all aboard," from the conductor, many a "good bye," "God bless you," from really sincere lips, and away rolled the train with its living freight, soon to be speeding northward to New York and the Centennial.

I was obliged to remain in Panama from the 15th to the 21st, before I found a steamer going further southward, which stay was more than sufficient to enable me to distinguish its peculiar features. Among these may be mentioned the wall fronting the bay, on which there is a smoothly paved promenade of several hundred yards length. This is a favorite place of resort immediately after sunset, for here the cooling sea breeze may be enjoyed uncontaminated with any of the city odours. Here also the view of Taboga and other islands to the southward, and of the mainland with its tropical growth, and ruins of the old city of Panama to the east, is magnificent. As night approaches, and the small, pale stars peep out, we become interested in observing the position of our northern constellations. The great Bear's "pointer" plainly show where the north star ought to be, but it is scarcely distinguishable in the haze of the horizon. As for Cassiopoeia, it has sunk down behind the earth altogether. Orion is brilliant in the northwestern sky, with Sirius in its wake. In the south, constellations, entirely new to a northern eye, are rising and setting. Among them is the Southern Cross, which, as it culminates, assumes something like the shape from which it derives its name. The star which forms its western shoulder is, however, too high, and destroys its symmetry, and the whole constellation cannot compare in brilliancy with any of our principal star groups of the north.

On the afternoon of the 21st I found myself on board the British steamer "Oroya," belonging to the South Pacific Steam Navigation Company, and bound for Callao. It is a vessel of 1,800 tons, built on the Clyde in 1873. It has side wheels, with a crank shaft driven directly from stationary cylinders by piston rods and connecting rods. The whole of this machinery is beneath the cranks, thus differing immensely from the "Montana," with its walking-beam towering above the upper deck. Then the "Montana" is built of wood and fitted up quite plainly. The "Oroya" is of iron, and most elaborately finished. But the latter is neither so cleanly kept nor so well ventilated as the "Montana." On this account the old ship smell, which I had so far escaped, on the Pacific, turns up like a familiar, but vulgar acquaintance, to annoy me. It is a pity that such a splendid ship should not be able to rid itself of such a pestilential nuisance. Scrupulous cleanliness in the steerage, and the total abolition of carpets and cushions aft, would, very probably, make the atmosphere of an ocean-going steamer as agreeable and *sweet* as that of any drawing-room.

At 10 o'clock on the evening of the 21st, the whistle was blown, the engines set in motion, the signal gun fired, and the "Oroya" turned her bows towards the Southern Cross, leaving the North Star to sink down beneath the horizon. Armstrong and I were the only cabin passengers on leaving Panama Bay. A few Spanish passengers came on board afterwards, but still we were left pretty much to our own resources, and must have felt rather lonely, but for the good company of the captain and officers of the "Oroya." Although in command of a British ship, Captain Hall was a native of the State of Maine, and a finer specimen could not well have been conceived of a down eastern skipper of the old school. Tall, broad and handsome, with iron grey hair and beard, and kindly blue eye; it was a pleasure to look at him as he strode the deck or sat at the head of the dinner table. This was at the end of the saloon furthest aft, the captain no doubt thinking, like a certain Highland Chief, that where he sat "was aye the head o' the table." The officers were mostly Scotchmen, and it was a great pleasure to me sometimes to indulge in a chat with them in "braid Scotch," and to recognize in my countrymen their native, strong, unassailable sound sense.

On Sunday, the 23rd April, I had occasion to observe another matter in which the "Oroya" compared disadvantageously with the "Montana." On board the American vessel service was read regularly every Sunday forenoon, while on the "Oroya," a British ship, nothing takes place to distinguish Sunday from any other day. It seems that the South Pacific Steam Navigation Company leave it to the decision of each captain as to whether he will hold service or not on board his ship, but Captain Hall, of the "Oroya," like Gallio, "cared for none of these things." The most of the officers seemed to be impregnated with the same indifference, and even scepticism, as the captain. There were, however, two exceptions, and the fact of their remaining true to their early convictions was plainly traceable to the influence of their religious education in Scottish parish schools. They were loud in their praises of educational matters in Scotland as they were twenty-five or thirty years ago, when the Bible and the proverbs of Solomon were text books, and the moral education in the school led on towards the higher spiritual discipline of the church. They thought that the men and women then reared in Scotland would compare advantageously with those who have enjoyed the benefits of modern systems, or even of the new Scottish Education Act. The latter decrees that "the time or times during which any religion is practiced, "or instruction in religious subjects is given, at any meet-"ing of the school for elementary instruction, shall be "either at the beginning or at the end of such meeting;" and that "any child may be withdrawn by his parents from "any instruction in religious subjects, and from any relig- "ious observance in the school." It thus leans plainly towards the establishment of the so-called "secular" system, according to which no religious instruction whatever is imparted to the scholars. In the course of our chat one of the Scotchmen, Campbell, exclaimed:

"Secular education! that is simply atheistical education, "for, twenty years ago, when I was in Glasgow, atheists of "the Holyoke school called themselves '*secularists*.'"

"I remember that well," said I, "and people ought to "recollect that there can be no neutrality in this matter; "that, where no religious instruction is given, irreligion or "atheism is practically taught."

"It is strange," said Finlayson, "that the Scotch, of all "nations, should forget that."

"The Scotch," said Armstrong, "are famous for quarrel- "ling among themselves, and forgetting the common enemy."

"They may get wiser," said Campbell, "and again take "up the fight against infidelity."

"I hope they may not lose it," said Armstrong, "in the "same manner as Culloden was lost to the Royalists, and "Bothwell Brig to the Covenanters."

I mentally prayed "amen." The fight on this question is not new in the world's history. It is the same as Calvin's battle with the "libertines" of his time, for too many influences in the present day tend "to confound together "heaven and earth, to destroy all religion whatsoever, to "efface all knowledge of the spiritual nature of man, to "deaden his conscience, and obliterate all distinction be- "tween men and brutes."*

---
* Guizot, St. Louis and Calvin.

THE PACIFIC COAST. 59

On the afternoon of the same Sunday we arrived at San Buenaventura after steaming up the Buenaventura river sixteen miles. The banks are low and clad with dense green wooding, and far beyond, to the southeast, a dark range of hills is seen with their summits hid in the clouds, behind which I was told lies Popayan, in the valley of the Cauca, a river which joins the Magdalena before their combined waters reach the Caribbean sea. This was my first glimpse of the Andes, those hills forming the most westerly of the three Cordilleras described by Humboldt as existing north of Ecuador. Hour after hour I watched those mountains, as the white clouds rolled along their dark sides and up their valleys, but a view of their highest part was denied me, and my first view of the Andes ended in disappointment. On shore I found Buenaventura to be a collection of dirty-looking huts, mostly built on piles and thatched with palm leaves. Even the church is built of no better material than the houses. The inhabitants are mostly negroes, dirty and half naked. Strangely contrasting with the general scene are groups of idle women, dressed in bright-colored fabrics, some of them young, and smoking cigars. In passing through the streets I was beset by deformed persons and ragged boys begging, and felt very contented when I found myself afloat again and on the way to the ship, which lay at anchor in the middle of the river.

The "Oroya" left San Buenaventura on the forenoon of the 24th, and shortly after we reached the Pacific, where a cool breeze from the west met us. This seemed to drive most of the clouds inland, leaving only a thick bank of cumulus hanging over the country immediately behind the shore. High above and beyond the rounded cumulus summits, dark blue mountain masses stood out from a gray clouded background, and here and there contrasted beautifully with the bright sun-lit cloud-tops beneath them. The whole line of the highest ridge was not unbroken by clouds, but in several places it was quite distinct, showing several peaks and hog-backed ridges. At other points it became faint, and disappeared as it rose into and pierced the dull, gray clouds of the background. At no point, however, were snow-tipped mountains observed, although the "frozen crest of the Andes" is mentioned by Prescott as having been visible to Pizarro from the Island of Gorgona, a few leagues farther to the south. This island and the coast near San Buenaventura was the scene of terrible sufferings on the part of Pizarro and his followers, during their earlier voyages in search of Peru. It was after dark when we passed Gorgona, where they had spent seven months of dreary wretchedness, three hundred and fifty years ago.

Next day we arrived at Tumaco, the neighbourhood of which has also been rendered classic by Prescott. Opposite lies the Island of Gallo, where Pizarro drew on the sand, with his sword, the famous line from east to west, and, followed by thirteen others, stepped to the south of it, choosing "Peru with its riches," rather than "Panama and its poverty." Tumaco is beautifully situated on a fertile island, the usual luxurious tropical undergrowth being relieved by the palm trees towering over it. These are not always beautiful, some of them being ragged and brown in the leaves, and resembling very tall umbrellas blown inside out. Associated with these are the square houses of bamboo laths, many of them built on posts about six feet high. Then come the natives, of every size, colour and costume. The latter is sometimes very scanty, and the whole scene resembles the pictures all of us have seen of tropical missionary stations. After inspecting Tumaco and once more regaining the ship, I felt tempted to exclaim with Bishop Heber—

"Every prospect pleases,
And only man is vile."

I fear, however, that, in spite of our boasted civilization, these lines have their application in temperate zones and Christian countries as well as in the tropics; and it must further be admitted that, in the latter, it applies to white as well as to black and yellow men. In Panama, for instance, there is not yet a Protestant church or meeting house, and the Europeans there patronize a cockpit, which many of them are not ashamed to visit on Sundays.

On the morning of the 26th April we arrived at Esmeraldas, a town situated at the mouth of a river of the same name, which takes its rise near Quito. It is the same described by Prescott as "the fair River of Emeralds, so "called from the quarries of the beautiful gem on its bor-"ders, from which the Indian monarchs enriched their "treasury." Another author mentions the emerald mine, but says: "I never visited it, owing to the superstitious "dread of the natives, who assured me that it was enchanted, "and guarded by an enormous dragon, which poured forth "thunder and lightning on those who dared to ascend the "river." Now, it is very strange, that, in spite of these two authorities, nothing whatever is known concerning the mine in question by the inhabitants of the place. They assured me that nothing of the kind had ever been worked in the neighborhood, and one of the more intelligent maintained that there was nothing, even in the shape of tradition, current concerning it. As for the hobgoblin story, I was unable to muster sufficient assurance to mention it. In all probability the emerald quarries never existed here, and the gems worn by the Indians, on the first arrival of the Spaniards, were most likely the product of an emerald mine near Bogota, the capital of New Granada, which is being worked to this day. At all these Pacific ports there are no wharves, and the steamer anchors in the rivers or roadsteads. The former have always very strong currents, and at Esmeraldas the anchorage is in twenty fathoms of water. The native boats and canoes come alongside to receive goods, and I was surprised at the facility with which they were loaded. This is owing to the "Oroya" being furnished with side hatches, which save much time in swinging over the goods. The canoes are "dugouts" of enormous size, some of them being forty feet long and five feet wide, with logs lashed to their sides to prevent capsizing.

By thus touching at a new port every day the "Oroya" left us but little time for chatting, unless in the evening, when I found it strange that the subject-matter of our conversations unfailingly gravitated towards education, and that the discussions on board the "Montana" should be continued on the "Oroya." But so it was, and such interest was manifested in them that they were even resumed on the quarter deck after dark, when the faces of the disputants could scarcely be seen, unless in the glow of the phosphorescent track which the steamer left immediately behind her in the water. And even here the American element was represented by the captain, who frankly "owned up" to the deterioration which had crept into the American social system since his boyhood. When pressed for his opinion as to the cause, he said, "It's all owing to "these cursed railroads."

"Well," said I, "*that* explanation *is* new to me."

"You see," he continued, "before they came into exist-
"ence our people were contented to lead a quiet, comfort-

"able life, on their farms or in the villages, but since then an inundation of well-dressed fops and glib-tongued bummers has spread over the country, and quite turned the heads of our boys and girls, who, every one of them, think that life outside of a city is annihilation almost."

"Don't you think, captain," asked Armstrong, "that ships and steamboats have to bear their share of the blame?"

"No sir," retorted the captain; "they carry a different class of passengers; serious, solid business people, who never harmed any community."

Whatever one may think of the captain's opinion, it is plain from it and from other utterances by "Montana" passengers that the American educational or training system is not at all in a satisfactory condition. The rising generation of the United States seem to be in the hands of a powerful but purposeless giant, who has no distinct aim for his arrows. It is to be feared that the greater number of these are aimed too low, and easily fall within the sphere of mundane and material influences, and that very few of them are aimed with such a force and in such a direction as will carry them into that higher light and life which is the real end and aim of our existence.

We crossed the equator on the night of the 26th, but no extraordinary event occurred such as frequently happened to sailing ships in old times. Old Neptune, it seems, disdains to pay visits to prosaic modern steamers, and no doubt would find some difficulty in scrambling on board. Next morning we touched at Manta, where we had visits from numerous hat pedlars, for it so happens that here and at Monte Christo and Jipijapa, in the interior, the famous so-called Panama hats are manufactured. This industry is confined exclusively to this part of Ecuador, where alone the wild grass grows which yields the raw material. All along the coast to Ballenita I watched anxiously for glimpses of the Andes, but they were either too far inland or the shore range was too high, or the weather too cloudy. It was not until after we entered the Gulf of Guayaquil, on the morning of the 28th, and sailed past the Island of Puna, that I descried to the eastward the dark wall of the Cordillera Cajas towering in huge masses high above the clouds. These mountains are, however, not more than forty miles distant, and beyond them, in the province of Quenca, the drainage is wholly towards the Atlantic. Strange that in this continent, over 2,000 miles broad, the watershed should approach so closely to its western edge. At Guayaquil itself it is very seldom that a glimpse of the mountains is to be obtained, and although it is said that Chimborazo sometimes shows himself, it must be, I think, on occasions few and far between.

After staying nearly two days at Guayaquil, we left on the 30th for Tumbez and Payta, at which latter port we arrived next morning. On the way we passed Santa Clara or El Muerto, an island which, at a distance, resembles a human body lying on its back. At Payta the rainless region of Peru begins, and as a consequence, the dense vegetation to which we had become accustomed disappears. Here it was that Pizarro first began to penetrate into the interior of the country, the forest having presented an impenetrable barrier at points further north. Payta is principally a coaling station for the South Pacific steamers. No green thing is here visible on shore, and the contrast with the banks of the Guayaquil is really startling. Water for the town is brought from a point twenty miles distant. Judging from the number of cattle brought to Payta for shipment, there must be some good agricultural districts in the interior. The mode of getting these cattle on board is worthy of notice. The chain from the marine derrick, which is used for loading ordinary merchandize, and which overhangs the *balsa* in which the cattle are brought alongside, is hooked round the horns of the poor beast, and the steam windlass soon lifts it off its feet. For a few seconds its whole weight is suspended in the air *by its horns;* then it is swung over and landed on the deck, *apparently* none the worse. But probably this would very much shock the good northern men who are on the alert to prevent cruelty to animals.

Payta is connected with Piura, a town in the interior, by a railway, which, however, is frequently drifted up by sand. The houses are the rudest of "shanties," but there is a well built custom house. Passengers for the steamer are, along the whole of this coast, almost always accompanied on board by a crowd of friends, who make the most affectionate demonstrations on leaving them.

From Payta the "Oroya's" course lay direct for Callao, taking us out of sight of land. This I could have borne, but the ocean was no longer pacific, and I spent two very uncomfortable days at the southern end of the journey, which reminded me of its uncomfortable commencement off San Francisco. But, after having spent twenty-eight days, and sailed 4,700 miles on Pacific waters, I thought, nevertheless, that I could felicitate myself on the good time I had spent, and on my safe arrival at Callao, which place we reached on the 3rd May. On approaching the coast another glimpse is obtained of the Andes, but quite as tantalizing as that we had off San Buenaventura. The mountains are almost invariably hidden in clouds, so that a clear view of them is seldom obtainable. Prescott describes Pizarro as navigating this coast with the Andes always in sight as his guide. If this really was the case, we must suppose that in those days they had exceptionally fine weather. Behind Callao, and close to the foot of the mountains, Lima is plainly distinguishable, with the towers of its cathedral bright and distinct.

In Callao I heard the cry of "hard times" on every hand, and certain facts thrust themselves upon my observation which indicated an extraordinary derangement of the financial affairs of Peru. American gold was at a premium of 77 1-2 per cent. in Peruvian paper currency. Peruvian "sols" commanded 37 per cent. premium. The "sol" (sun) is a silver coin almost equivalent to a Canadian dollar in value. One hears nothing of the old gold dollar (peso de oro) used by the Spaniards, and although, judging from the name, the modern Peruvians seem to have returned to the worship of the "sun," they are not rich enough to provide images in the proper metal. The Peruvian "sol," being of silver, ought to be called a "moon" rather than a "sun." But after all it does not make much matter, since all their "suns" are made of paper. These are irredeemable legal tenders, and silver and gold were being exported in large quantities in payment of foreign indebtedness. This caused the government to take alarm and *prohibit* the exportation of silver, and at the time of my visit it had to be *smuggled* out of the country. Passengers and others on board the Pacific Steam Navigation Company's steamers were buying silver in Callao with American gold, obtaining 26 per cent. premium. The silver they sold in Panama for gold, paying only 15 per cent., thus making a clear profit of 11 per cent. Meanwhile custom house officers were searching the vessels and passengers' baggage as they left Callao, *confiscating all the specie*, the government remaining under the delusion that by this means they could stop its outflow. Peru is far behind with the payment of interest on its bonds in London. The revenue from guano sales is growing less. Indeed, people say that the good guano is all gone, and that there are not a million tons of inferior quality left. Extravagance, corruption and "logrolling" have here, as in other republics, produced their legitimate fruits.

It is also said that ill-advised railway building has contributed not a little to bring about this disastrous state of affairs. From Pacasmayo, Chimbote, Lima, Mollendo, and other places on the coast, expensive railways have been built into the interior, in some cases crossing the Andes at a height of 15,000 feet. Probably not less than $100,000,000 have been expended in this way, and scarcely any of the lines are finished. All construction upon them has been stopped, and, of course, until they are completed, they can not bring any revenue to the government. Many believe that, even after completion, they will never pay, being very expensive to run, and mostly constructed through districts which will yield them no traffic. It might be well if people elsewhere would "look before they leap" in this matter of railway building. In opening up a new country one must take risks, but in a country already "opened," it is surely necessary to enquire beforehand whether it can support a railway.

But there are other political doctors who don't blame the railways. "How comes it," asks one of them, "that this " country, with an area ten times that of England, has only " the population of pigmy Switzerland?" Here is the cause, according to the same writer: " The enemy of Peru " is an old enemy of mankind. It is, and always has been " and always will be, the most tyrannical, most aggressive, " most oppressive, most cruel and most selfish element in "the moral world. Need I say that this wicked monster is "Religion?" This is no doubt plain speaking and very radical, but I must say that in no country is there less religion visible. There is, on the one hand, superstition, to which the natives are subject, and on the other, unbelief, or blank secularism, which has taken hold of the foreigners, but Christian men, with the fear of God before their eyes, seem scarce enough in Peru.

In spite of all this the people seem happy, and always on the look out for amusement. The 2nd of May was the anniversary of the bombardment of Callao by the Spaniards in 1866. The Peruvians claimed it as a victory, and therefore there had been a grand fete on the day previous to our arrival, which was continued on the 3rd, with fire-works and gas illumination. What they have to rejoice about is not very clear, for the Spaniards did as they pleased and then went away. There was a great turnout of all classes, for all dearly love a fete and fire-works. Extravagant dresses seemed to be the exception among the ladies. A few sported Parisian fashions, and some negro women with cigars in their mouths, and impregnable complexions, carried handsome silk parasols. But the women generally wore the "panuelon," or light shawl of black merino over their heads and dresses. In the case of ladies, it was of fine quality and fringed with black lace; with poorer women it was of coarse material, but all wore it, although in some cases the underdress might only consist of a shift and petticoat.

Peru is rainless, and the houses of Callao are frequently roofless, and have not even boards laid over the joists and plaster of the ceilings. The walls of the meaner houses consist of cane laths, with mud plastered on the outside. Some have no covering whatever, but these are mostly in the outskirts of the city. European influence is apparent in the handsome wharves that line the harbor, in the gas-lighted streets, and in the numbers of Scotch and English workmen who throng them. Passing along one of the streets in the centre of the city, in the evening, I heard very distinctly the strains of the old Scotch psalm tune, "Martyrdom." They came from a building not at all like a church. I entered, but found only the choir assembled in a place of worship evidently Episcopal. They sang afterwards—

> "The Church's one foundation
> Is Jesus Christ our Lord."

reminding me very forcibly of a certain small village church far away in the north. On inquiry I found that the church was principally supported by the Pacific Mail Steam Navigation Company for the benefit of the workmen employed in their machine shops. There are about four hundred hands, but they are principally Scotch, and little disposed to attend the Church of England. Like the Macdonalds at Culloden and the Highland regiments in the Peninsula, they retain their old national obstinacy, and are indisposed to waive any of their prejudices for the sake of the common good. Unhappily, too, the national vice is indulged in, and whiskey ruins, it is said, a larger proportion of Scotchmen in Callao than even in the old country.

On the 4th of May Armstrong and I visited Lima, which, had it been built in modern days, would probably have been named Pizarroville. I am not conceited enough to describe it from the experiences of one day. Previous to leaving Callao on the day following, I learnt that a seizure had recently been made of 2,000 sols, and therefore exchanged all mine for gold coins of Ecuador and Columbia. I turned my face northward with great satisfaction, and thoroughly enjoyed the beautiful weather, pacing the deck of the "Santiago," until the towers of Lima, the masts of Callao and the bold Island of San Lorenzo had melted away in the mists of the Pacific.

III.—THE CORDILLERAS.

" Which shaketh the earth out of her place, and the pillars thereof tremble." Job ix, 6.

I returned to Guayaquil on the 10th May, and occupied myself with the business which had occasioned my journey to South America. In attending to it I very soon learned that the Republic of Ecuador, otherwise so penurious, indulges in the luxury of a State Geologist, although it neither supplies him with an assistant, a museum nor a laboratory. I very gladly waited upon this gentleman, who proved to be Dr. Theodore Wolf, lately Professor of Geology in Quito, formerly of Bonn, the friend and correspondent of Gustav Rose and Vom Rath, and the author of the very interesting geological communications from Ecuador published in the Journal of the German Geological Society, and in the New Year Book for Mineralogy. He accorded me a hearty reception, disinterested advice, lively personal assistance, and seemed overjoyed, in the midst of an alien and unsympathising population, to meet a colleague, even of the humblest description, and to converse with him, in his own language, on subjects of mutual interest. He furnished me with notes directing my attention to the points of greatest geological interest to be seen on my proposed journey into the interior, and even volunteered to assist me in the purchase of a riding outfit (*montura*), indispensable for my trip across the mountains. When I took him at his word, he quickly donned his soutane (for he was a Roman Catholic priest as well) and strode with me through the streets to various stores, where

I rapidly became the owner of a saddle and bridle, stirrups like large brass slippers, and intended to enclose the whole foot; spurs with formidable rowels, like little circular saws; a bit, consisting of the largest mouthful of iron I had ever seen imposed upon a horse, and a waterproof *poncho*, after the fashion of the country.

"But you must have water-proof leggings as well," said the doctor.

"For the rain?"

"No, for the mud; you will see."

"Very well," said I, resignedly, although they seemed to me quite superfluous.

The course of the River Guayaquil is almost due north and south, and it receives the whole drainage of the western slope of the Andes, from the peaks of Illiniza southward past Quirotoa and Chimborazo to the mountains of the Province of Alausi. But the watershed is seldom distant more than 100 miles from the waters of the Pacific, and east of this limit all the rivers find their way to the Amazon and the Atlantic. The route towards the pass of Chimborazo leads first northward on the river from Guayaquil to Bodegas, about seventy miles. Two small, primitive-looking steamers, having their boilers and engines exposed to full view on the deck, ply on the river, leading very irregular lives, having no stated hours, or even days, for performing their duties. On board one of these, the "Quito," I left Guayaquil, on the morning of the 13th May, for the interior. The river is broad and swift, and the tide sweeps up and down for forty miles, doing most of the carrying trade for the lazy inhabitants along the banks. Schooners, boats or barges are very scarce, balsas and canoes being mostly employed. The banks of the river are low, and covered to the edge with densest wooding. Now and then we pass beautiful *haciendas*, or farms, with their magnificent tropical foliage of plantain and banana groves, bread-fruit and cocoa trees, coffee bushes and sugar-cane. These contrast favorably with the ricketty and dirty-looking buildings, and the groups of idle negroes and tawdry negresses around them. Sometimes we pass, at a distance from the river, picturesque hills, isolated, and clothed with dense vegetation to their summits. As we go northward the river begins to resemble a canal with steep banks of deep alluvium, which it is constantly undermining. Here and there a low bank is seen, with alligators sunning themselves, just like motionless, dirty logs, and lazily resuming their watery element as the steamer approaches. Deep and rich is the soil, and many a vicissitude is it exposed to from the inundations which the rushes of water from the mountains occasion. Sometimes there is seen, at a depth of six or eight feet beneath the surface, a stratum of black earth, intermixed with pieces of old pottery and tiles, telling a tale of prehistoric times and modes of living, which it would be interesting indeed to listen to. But we had to listen instead to very prosaic conversation on board the steamer about the cocoa crop, the scarcity of labour, and the laziness of the negroes. Among the passengers is a Columbian, from New Granada, very lively considering his circumstances, for he says he is an old soldier and is going to his home near Popayan, a place far north of Quito, and evidently has very little money in his pocket or clothes on his back. We arrived at Bodegas in the afternoon, and found it to be, as its name implies, a mere collection of huts and storehouses for goods on their way to Quito.

Next morning I made a start on my inland ride, and was doomed to take leave of Armstrong and the few persons who, up to this point, had conversed with me in broken

English. In saying "good bye," I remembered that I was cutting loose from the last traces of civilization, and felt like going out to sea with unproved compass and unreliable crew. In consonance with my feelings, I mounted my mule and rode very quietly out of the village, the baggage mule and peon following. Other travellers (natives) do not make their exit or entrée so modestly, but arrive or leave at a canter, and with a most ostentatious dash and splash. A few hours companionship with the peon inspired me with confidence, for I found that my Spanish was far from being useless. I had begun the study of the language on leaving San Francisco, and now, on putting my acquirements to the actual test, was satisfied with my progress. The peon was very polite, but he no longer called me señor, sir; I was the patron, master. Peon in Spanish is a day labourer, or footsoldier, but the name is generally used in South America to indicate the man who travels on foot with the mules, loads and unloads, and has charge of them.

Quite unexpectedly, as we were leaving Bodegas, my Columbian acquaintance of the day before joined our cavalcade. He was not troubled with any baggage, and fell into the ranks with the peon and the mules. In ten minutes after leaving Bodegas we had lost sight of it, and were in full enjoyment of a ride on the highroad to Quito. I had previously seen at Bodegas many of the peons from the interior as they arrived, and remarked that their linen trousers were invariably rolled up as far as possible on their thighs, and now the Columbian rids himself of shoes and stockings and gets into the same trim as the peon. The reason soon becomes plain, and, at the same time, I understand why Dr. Wolf recommended leggings. It is all to face and fathom the bottomless mud which we have to encounter, in quantity and adhesiveness far surpassing anything I have seen on the worst footpath of a Canadian backwood. I found that the end nearest Guayaquil of the route leading from the chief seaport of Ecuador to the capital has been laid out and trodden down, exclusively by the mules and peons, and is not entitled to be called a road. Dense tropical woods close in upon it, with their growth coming as much from above as below. Sometimes the mass of foliage overhead is so dense that the light has great difficulty in penetrating, and the road seems to lie in a tunnel of vegetation, the bright sunlight streaming in at each end. At other times the forests open into wide park-like pastures, where the track splits up into numerous little footpaths. Here we usually pass *hacienda* buildings and fences, with the never-failing banana groves. But we also encounter in these open spaces ditches and pools of water from ten to twenty yards wide, through which the mules and peons have to struggle.

About midday we reached Palmar, where there is a bridge across the Babahoyo. After passing it the road becomes dry and sandy, and leads past cocoa plantations, where lie heaps of their yellow shells rifled of their fruit in the recent harvest. I enquire for a place to dine, but obtain no satisfaction, and come to understand that neither mules nor men in this country expect to eat or rest, unless in the morning and evening. I console myself with the expectation of good fare and quarters on reaching Playas. The cocoa trees gradually give place to the densest forest, and the sandy road to the deepest of mud. Hangers and creepers grow more numerous, and encroach upon the path which narrows to about three feet wide. The mules seek the driest places at the side, and my hat and clothes are brought into conflict with the branches, and come off much damaged. But the sides become as bad as the middle of the path, and nothing remains for the animals but to go right through the centre of the frightful puddle, which they very patiently do. The structure of the pathway becomes remarkable ; in places where the water does not quite gain the upper hand, I discern ruts not running parallel with, but across the road. These are formed by the mules placing their feet conscientiously in the tracks of their predecessors. The ruts extend with great regularity quite across the pathway, even where it widens out to ten or twelve feet. So do also the intervening ridges, developing a sort of corduroy structure, and made up not of logs but of mud, more or less dry. The ridges seem, however, to be of some service in supporting the body of the animal while his feet are searching for bottom in the ruts. This may provoke a smile, but it is no exaggeration, for my stirrups frequently scraped on the ridges in passing over them. As if this were not enough, ditches present themselves, which I can only cross dry shod by getting my feet up on the mule's neck and holding on desperately by the saddle.

The road occasionally touches the river, which becomes more turbulent, for both are nearing the mountains, glimpses of which we sometimes obtain through the foliage and the clouds. It is now late in the afternoon, and rain begins. I find my rain poncho invaluable, but the peon and Columbian are both soaked. The reputed old soldier is thoroughly worn out, and cries, "O, my companion, I shall die." Fortunately for him, we encounter an old horse out grazing, which he borrows without the owner's leave, and then abandons as we approach Playas. This place we reach at dusk, just as I was beginning to fear we would have to camp in the woods. But no comfortable quarters await us. The peon stops and unloads his animals in the lower flat of a common looking house at the roadside, inhabited by negroes. In the upper story we hear the family talking, who, in spite of the Columbian's eloquence, have determined to do nothing for us, but advise us to go elsewhere. This the peon will not do, and I don't like the idea of going on a wild goose chase after better quarters. We therefore spend the night on the ground floor, damp and comfortless, but not entirely supperless. Francisco, the peon, shares his soup with me, and I try to improvise a bed with my saddle for a pillow. But, without light, my efforts were vain at arranging such a couch as would invite sleep, and visits during the night from mosquitoes, pigs and dogs, effectually frightened off " Nature's sweet restorer."

Next morning (the 15th) we left Playas on empty stomachs. The poor Columbian, whose feet were very much scratched and swollen, had succeeded in driving a bargain with a muleteer who was returning to the mountains with a lame horse. For a small sum, which I volunteered to contribute, he obtained the use of the animal as far as Guaranda. Mounted, he and I bear a distant resemblance to Sancho Panza and Don Quixote, and our party forms a somewhat comic-looking cavalcade travelling at a very modest pace. In this respect we are very much unlike other travellers in these regions. As we toil along quietly, these riders tear past us at full gallop, with arms, legs and *ponchos* swinging about, and the spurs continually digging into the sides of the poor horses. Truly, the Spaniard is neither merciful to his beast nor to himself,—and as to his baggage, it is left to follow at its leisure or that of the peon who has it in charge. The character of the road does not seem to be in the slightest degree considered, and over rock or mud the animals are urged to the utmost of their speed.

After leaving Playas we get over several miles of bottomless road, and then it enters a boulder region and winds in among, over and around huge masses of rock, between which the careful mule has much difficulty in finding footing. Where there is any soil between the stones it is worked up into corduroy ruts like those of yesterday. But we have the beginning of the Andes in view, and also the gorge from which issues the Cristal river, and through which our road lies. We enter the gorge or glen, and have to cross the river several times, by fording, at places where the current seems strong enough to carry away both mule and rider. Afterwards the road keeps to the north side of the glen, and improves as it ascends the hillsides, for the mules have been able to avoid the boulder ground and there is very little flat country. About noon, we came in sight of a likely-looking cottage in the midst of a group of banana and orange trees. Here we were successful in obtaining some potato soup and round flat cakes such as a Scot would call scones. For dessert we suggested oranges, and obtained them off the trees, carrying a supply with us. Payment for the oranges was refused; "They are worth nothing," was the remark. In all our intercourse with the natives the Columbian seemed to fancy himself an interpreter, and interfered betwixt said natives and myself, merely repeating their words to me in a louder key, as if I had been a little deaf. But he was good company, and never tired of talking, as if I had not the slightest difficulty in understanding him.

As we progress eastward the sides of the glen become steeper, but are still covered with foliage, and little or no rock is visible unless in the beds of some of the side streams which we cross. Like the most of the boulders below, the rock in place consists of greenstone varieties and of green-coloured schists. In most places deep alluvium—here very fertile, there very stony—covers up the rocks. Orange and banana gardens and maize fields are quite frequent, and after passing Palsabamba a very decided improvement takes place in the road. The river splits up into two branches, and we cross the most northern of these, but this time on a good log bridge. Further on we perceive, for the first time, that human skill and labour have been employed to plan and cut out a road in a zigzag direction up the steep sides and edge of the hill lying betwixt the two valleys. The road is excavated in a kaolin bed, evidently the result of the decomposition *in situ* of the underlying granitic rock. The rock itself is only seen at points few and far between, for the clay bed is twenty to forty feet thick, but the mica is distributed through the kaolin just as in the unaltered rock. The road is good, becomes more and more picturesque, the zigzagging gives new prospects at every turn, and for the first time since I started on my ride I begin to enjoy it. As the afternoon wears on, and as we follow these zigzag paths, ever ascending, the banks into which they are cut becoming steeper and steeper, clouds collect among the hills, and rain descends in the form of a Scotch mist.

As it began to grow dark my talk with the peon became very animated as to the whereabouts of the stopping place or *casa de posada*, for I was anxious to avoid the experience of the previous night. Every cottage that comes in view is closely scanned. The Columbian frequently engages the inmates in conversation and proposes half-a-dozen times to dismount for the night, but the peon urges us to go further, with the promise of better quarters and a better landlady— a *muy buena patrona*. At nightfall we reached Puzo, where I found the horsemen, who had passed us so hurriedly in the morning, quartered for the night. They were very polite and talkative, one of them, who was styled by the others the "Commandant," shewing very much interest in the object of my journey. He commiserated me when I told him of my bad fortune the preceding night, and recommended me, on my return, to stay at the house of a certain Señor Pablo Hurtado. All of us occupied the upper story of the house, which was open on two sides and sheltered on the west and north. Here, after a supper of potato soup, we obtained a good night's rest, although the bamboo boards were hard and rough and our supply of blankets scanty.

I was awakened next morning before dawn by the chatter of the peons while loading their mules and taking their departure, some going higher up the mountains and some towards the Guayaquil lowlands. It is still moonlight, and the dark outlines of the first story of the Andes rise around us, while away down, in the valley we passed through, lies a dense bank of white cloud. The day dawns, we breakfast as best we can on potatoes and eggs, and make a start in our quiet, steady way. The mule path pursues the same zigzag course, the soil is deep and rich and luxuriant crops of maize surround some of the cottages which we pass. The brows and peaks of the mountains come out more distinctly as little by little we overtop them,—and at every turn new views, each more beautiful and magnificent than the other, develope themselves. From a height of 8,000 feet we look down towards the west on the low hills we have surmounted, all clothed with dense green forest, and beyond them, dimly seen through the haze, is the Guayaquil valley. At our feet nestle valleys with their bright green spots of grove and garden and white bands of foamy rivers. Rocky cliffs show themselves now and then in the mountain sides, and the road is sometimes carried up alongside of them. Roughly schistose greenstones prevail after passing out of the granite district of yesterday. Higher and higher we go, still zigzagging, one part of the road following almost perpendicularly above the other, so that it would be an easy matter, in places, to spit down on the mules toiling up behind us.

At last the zigzagging is finished, and a long stretch of the road is seen bearing away to the southward and gradually rising to what appears to be the summit of the range. We do not follow it, however, but, on the demand of the peon, strike off to the left up into the old steep path trodden out naturally by countless mules and their *cargas* during past centuries. I begin to fear a repetition of the first day's miseries, for the mud corduroy reappears, varied here and there by bottomless puddles. But there are no rocks, and for long stretches the road has been worn down into deep black soil, until a section of it would represent the letter U, the walls on each side being frequently as high as mule and rider combined. The great disadvantage of this formation of road is that its bottom consists of well-wrought clay, so tough that as the poor mule withdraws its leg and hoof a sound is heard at each step like the uncorking of a very large bottle. But, to compensate for all this, the path gradually becomes less steep, then level, so that it is plain we have surmounted the first story of the Andes. Then we reach open spaces in the forest, through which it is very pleasant riding. The high trees and dense growth disappear and their place is supplied by rather high bushes, among which we can discern myrtles and fuchsias—the latter in full flower. Little by little even these disappear, the road begins to descend, and gradually there opens out before us, to the east, a wide expanse of hill and valley, with pasture, grass, and cultivated fields. These reach almost to the summit of the hills, and are divided into irregular patches by strips of wooding, which also usually crowns the hill tops.

As we journey eastward we descend into a valley and cross a busy brook at the bottom, which runs to the southeastward, watering flocks and turning little mills in a very primitive fashion as it goes. Then we gradually ascend the north side of the valley, where the enormous depth and evident fertility of the soil is astonishing. It may also be observed that the sides of the valley seem to be divided into small lots running parallel with it, all cultivated and rising one above another like so many stories, each with its line of little straw-thatched cottages with their gables turned towards the stream. As we mount the northern side of the valley, we suddenly turn into a recess in it where lies the village of Chapacoto.

The ride from this place to Guaranda is one of the most tantalising, although passing in view of the most magnificent scenery. The path leads over the ridge which separates the tributaries of the Babahoyo from those of the Yaguachi, and along the northwest side of the valley of the Chimbo, but is interrupted by numerous deep ravines or *quebradas*, the descent into and ascent from which would seem almost impracticable for any other animals except mules. The hills which separate these valleys and gorges are all cultivated, shew no rock outcrops whatever, but an enormous thickness of deep rich loam covered with crops of peas, beans, corn, wheat, and oats. The fences consist of earthwork (or adobe blocks) or rows of bushes or cactus. In pasturing animals, they are usually tethered, and the pigs seem to perform useful work in rooting over the field, piece by piece. They are certainly the longest-nosed swine I ever saw, and I imagine that this extraordinary development of snout is owing to its being so much in request as an agricultural implement. This would, at least, seem the correct explanation according to Darwin. But indeed the snouts would seem to be quite as effective as the plough in common use, which here consists mainly of a pointed wooden stake. The fields of grain and pasture spread like a variegated patchwork far and wide over hill and valley, and stretch away up into the mountains of the Western Cordillera, ridge upon ridge of which rises to the eastward, piercing the clouds, so that the highest peaks are invisible. At this point I was forcibly reminded of Church's picture, "The Heart of the Andes," and the piling up of mountain upon mountain which it exhibits, and an approach to which I had never before witnessed. Nor had I ever before seen anything to equal the magnificent beauty and extent of the cultivated landscape, and never before realised the grandeur of the Psalmist's expression, "The cattle on a thousand hills," for it would have been an easy matter to count that number in the panorama around.

On nearing Guaranda the tops of the mountains to the eastward are observed to be more rugged, but the protruding rocks are not jagged or peaked but rather of a rounded and warty character. Before reaching the town we descend into another deep *quebrada*, at the bottom of which the Rio Salinas, the main source of the Chimbo and Yaguachi, is spanned by a stone bridge with beautiful, elliptical arch. In descending to the river we join the new road which we parted from in the morning, and which improves in workmanship as we penetrate into the interior. It is paved across a width of about twenty feet by smooth round boulders from the river, most of which are dark-colored and consist of various greenstone species. Late in the afternoon we reach Guaranda, a town of about 10,000 inhabitants, and for the first time since leaving Guayaquil I enjoy the luxury of a room, a bed, and a civil landlord. Here we rejoin the Commandant, who had parted from us in the morning. The equipment of the hotel has an antiquated appearance, and we are waited on at table by a one-eyed attendant in a hat and red poncho, whose aspect reminds me of Mephistopheles as usually seen on the German stage.

When on the point of starting next morning I was surprised to find my baggage-mule loaded, not only with my own effects, but with a huge trunk besides. I found that this belonged to another traveller, and I objected to carrying it unless one-half of the hire of the animal to Ambato were deducted. The contractor, from whom I had hired the animals the previous evening, declined to reduce either the fare or the load. I then ordered the mule to be unloaded, and Mephistopheles took my baggage up to my room again. Next followed negotiations, absorbing much time and talk, in which both the "Commandant" and the Columbian took my side of the dispute quite warmly. At last my opponent gave in, loaded the mule with my baggage only, politely assisted me to mount, but muttered, at the same time, that I was a cursed "gringo." But I laughed, bade him good day, and rode out of the courtyard of the *casa de posada*. This term *gringo* is applied all along the South Pacific coast to North Americans and Europeans, and is said to have originated at the opening of the Lima & Callao Railway, many years ago. On this occasion the workmen employed on the line had a holiday and an excursion. Seated on the open railway waggons, passing through Callao, they sang "Green grows the rashes O" very lustily, confining themselves almost exclusively to the refrain of the song. The natives are said thereupon to have caught up the two first words and corcorrupted them into "gringo" as a nickname for the Europeans. So much is at any rate certain that it is a word thoroughly incorporated into the Spanish of the Pacific coast, and I have even heard the diminutives *gringito* and *gringita* applied to a little boy or girl of supposed European origin.

We left Guaranda on the morning of the 17th May. Its altitude, according to Reiss and Stubel, is 8,750 feet, and very little increase of height is gained for the first half day's riding after leaving it. There are several rivers to cross, each lying at the bottom of a deep gorge, with the usual precipitous descent to and ascent from them. The roads are always paved at the very steep places near the rivers, which are all Chimbo tributaries,—and even at the last one closest to the Cordillera the waterworn stones used are still small and fine grained greenstones, some of them with streaks of epidote. The mountain tops were hidden in the clouds, and the weather again became threatening. The last valley we crossed is broader than the others, and herds of cattle were pasturing in it. Some horsemen were endeavouring to catch some of the animals, and their expertness with the lasso I very much admired. In the same valley the road passes over the debris of a huge landslide which has come down from the adjacent steep mountain, and which seems to consist of volcanic material having the appearance of the small slag, or schlackenklein, on a furnace-house floor.

At last we have crossed the last ridge and scaled the side of the last *quebrada*, and the real ascent of the Western Cordillera begins. Our route follows the south side of a glen, at the bottom of which a Chimbo tributary flows westward. The road is notched out of the side of the glen, and zigzags upwards for hour after hour. The weather becomes thicker, the fog hiding every thing except the white band of foam at the bottom of the glen. Then, as a histologist would say, the impalpable fog graduates into fine-grained Scotch mist, and that again into small-grained rain. The road is cut into deep black soil, is here and there paved, but, as we get up further, the paving gives way to rows of angular stones placed diagonally across the road. These stones are derived from rock in situ at the side of the road, which consists of granular and slaty greenstones. As we ascend, the warty protuberances of rock, seen from beyond Guaranda, are discerned through the mist fringed with uncouth looking pines. Some of these rock exposures I visited on descending, and was struck with the brecciated character of some of them, which, as well as the greenstones and green slates, reminded me of certain Huronian rocks. As we slowly ascended the mountain side the showers became heavy and frequent, and at last a thunderstorm prevailed. This caused us to take refuge in a small hut, which I afterwards learned was a locality dignified with the name Panzas, and the altitude of which had been determined by Reiss and Stubel at 13,530 feet. The rain descended in torrents, even through the roof of the hut, which became crowded with refugees. Two Indian women of the better class, travelling westward on horseback, also sought shelter, and this obliged us to take to the road again, although the storm had not abated. My mule objected to facing the rain, and succeeded in throwing me off, but I soon got into the saddle and forced her to face the mountain again.

At Panza all attempts at road-making seem to have

ceased, but as the upper layer of black soil is mostly washed away, the mules find good footing in the underlying volcanic material. The mule path still ascends what is called the *paramo* (wilderness or heath) that forms the shoulders of the Cordillera, and we at last reach a broad ridge, more or less flat and about half a mile across, whitened with recently fallen hail, which is evidently the arenal or pass of Chimborazo, but nothing is seen of the higher peaks, which are shrouded in mist. On the left, and turning northward, is the valley by which we ascended, and as we trot eastward the falling rain extemporises little streamlets, which now flow with us and tell us that we have crossed the watershed of the continent, which here has an altitude of 14,040 feet. But the consideration at the moment is not particularly impressive, for the rain is pouring down, and we urge our mules to a trot, as the road now begins to descend. We hurry down along the paths, which resemble great black ruts, and past rocks of a lighter colour and different character from the monotonous greenstones and slates. The little rills which travel with us soon join a considerable brook, and form one of the small beginnings of the mighty river which, after travelling 4,000 miles eastward, reaches the Atlantic. Crossing the new-born tributary of the Amazon we reach a solitary house of adobe blocks called Tortorillas, and, wet and weary, gladly find shelter there. The Columbian is wet to the skin and shivering with cold, but contrives to warm himself a very little at the diminutive fire which the good patrona kindles under her earthen pots. This place (Tortorillas) is 12,820 feet high, or 1,220 feet lower than the ridge of the Cordillera which we have just crossed.

Next morning, at "peep of day," my first impulse is to step outside and reconnoitre the weather. The mist is rising on the hills, and breaks are visible in the clouds overhead, which are drifting rapidly westward. Soon the sunlight converts the grey vapour into dazzling white, which contrasts beautifully with the patches of deep blue sky. But I suddenly become aware that some of the dazzling white does not move, and, as the real clouds clear away, I discern the huge snow-clad dome of Chimborazo towering on high, its summit reaching nearly 8,000 feet higher than the spot where I stand. Thin, fleecy clouds are flitting around and adhering to it, resembling the hoary locks of an old man's head fluttering in the breeze. Here and there, at the base of the dome, rugged rocks are seen projecting through the snow, but higher up nothing mars its beautiful white, which seems to possess a slightly greenish tint. Long after we mount and start I never tire looking at the magnificent mountain, which, according to Reiss and Stubel's measurement, is 20,700 feet high. During the previous evening we had crossed the left shoulder of Chimborazo, supposing the mountain to be facing westward. After becoming familiar with its various aspects, I begin to invest it with fanciful personality. Although very rugged in places, the great dome has the shape of an old-fashioned wideawake, tapering rather too suddenly upwards, but well-rounded off at top. The hat alone is snow-covered, and its rim, turned down, seems to conceal a very thick neck. It is so large as to come right down upon the shoulders of the old man, who is in a sitting posture, looking towards the Pacific. Guaranda and Chapacoto lie in his lap, his knees form the ridge above Puzo, and his feet stretch away down to Playas, in the Guayaquil deepland. We cannot see his features, for we are now riding over *paramos* and across *quebradas*, behind his back, to the eastward.

Gradually we emerge from the mountain defiles beneath Chimborazo, and gradually there opens before us a magnificent view of the central Andean valley of Riobamba, and beyond it, thirty miles distant, rises the dark ridge of the Eastern Cordillera, its upper outline stretching like a huge chain through the clouds. Gradually, also, the full significance of this term *Cordillera* dawns upon us. It does not mean the immense collection of mountain chains, peaks, volcanoes, and *paramos*, called the Andes, but is applied chiefly to two of the principal ridges which give form and character to the whole of the enormous aggregate. Like a huge wall, darkened here and there by great recesses and with a pretty uniform height of 13,000 feet, the Eastern Cordillera runs from north to south, and out of it, isolated and, as it were, distinct altogether from the Cordillera, rise the snow-clad peaks for which the Andes are so famous.

The only one of these visible from our present standpoint is the celebrated Capac Urcu, king of mountains, regarding which Humboldt, in his Cosmos, relates that it is said to have been formerly an active volcano and to have exceeded Chimborazo in height, but that it fell in and became extinct in the latter part of the fifteenth century, fourteen years before the capture of Quito by the son of the Inca, Tupac Yupanqui. The appearance of the mountain certainly lends color to this tradition. It consists of several sharp snow peaks, all leaning towards the same centre and pointing to the imaginary apex which must have existed in old times according to the legend. But like many other pretty stories, this one too seems fated to melt away before the uncompromising light of modern research. According to Wolf, the Indians named, and still name the mountain Collanes, the altar,—but Capac Urcu is a name altogether unknown in its neighbourhood, and seems to have originated with Humboldt. Even the tradition of its falling in does not exist at present among the natives, and the cultivated people of Ecuador first heard of it from Humboldt's works. It seems that Humboldt, somewhat too credulously, took the word of a single individual, an Indian zebla in Riobamba, for the story of the existence of the tradition in question.

After following the river which comes down from Chimborazo, and which is called the Rio San Juan, we cross it and bear away to the north. The river itself runs down towards Riobamba; in fact, the road over the Chimborazo pass leads into the valley of that name,—and the streets of the town itself are seen in the distance, taking the shape of six small parallel bands brighter than the surrounding country. It lies in the midst of a cultivated valley, but the fields have not the same bright colour as those around Chapacoto and Guaranda. They seem to be less moist and have a greenish-gray colour, but they are equally extensive, and stretch away up into the mountains south of Riobamba, culminating in the Nudo di Pomachaca. The term Nudo, literally knot, knuckle or joint, is a very significant one in Andean nomenclature. While the Cordilleras, or chains, usually extend in a north and south direction, and are the main ridges of the Andes, the *nudos*, or knots, most frequently run across from east to west, combining the two main Cordilleras, and separating the hollow lying between them into distinct basin-shaped depressions such as the Germans call "Kesselthaler," or cauldron valleys. Thus, there may be distinguished, from south to north successively, the central valleys of Loja, Alansi, Riobamba, Ambato, Tacunga, Quito, and Ibarra, all lying between the Eastern and Western Cordilleras, and separated from each other by cross ranges, knots, or nudos.

The drainage and rivers of these central valleys sometimes break through the Eastern, sometimes through the Western Cordillera, and make their way in opposite directions to the Atlantic or the Pacific. The rivers collecting in the valleys of Riobamba and Ambato form ultimately the Rio Pastassa, which finds its way eastward through a deep gorge at Baños, near the foot of the volcano Tunguragua.

The name Riobamba is familiar to many, and must awaken sombre recollections as regards the devastations consequent upon violent earthquakes. The great earthquake which destroyed the town of Riobamba took place on the 4th February, 1797. Perhaps more has been written about this earthquake than about all the other earthquakes of Ecuador put together. Its unusual celebrity is owing to the circumstance that Humboldt visited the spot five years after it happened, collected all the information he could obtain concerning it, and incorporated it in his works. According to Wolf, however, the great traveller was very much misled by the inaccuracies and exaggerations of the natives. Instead of 40,000, there could not have been more than 5,000 or 6,000 killed. Six thousand is the highest estimate for the whole Province of Riobamba, while the actually ascertained deaths only amounted to 2,036. All this is quite satisfactory, and, on the whole, this earthquake does not seem to have been the most violent ever experienced in Ecuador. That of the 16th August, 1868, which devastated the Province of Imbabura, in the north, was far more violent and destructive.

Leaving the road to Riobamba on our right, we turn northward across the nudo, or cross range, separating the valley of Riobamba from that of Ambato. This range is called the Cerro Ygualata, and, at first, interrupts our view of the northern continuation of the Eastern Cordillera.

But to the left we are, now and then, favoured with views of Chimborazo, and gradually his younger brother, Carihuirazo, comes into view. It consists of an irregular, long-drawn ridge, also snow-covered, with an elevation of 16,750 feet. Our road is over the *paramos*, in the usual black ruts, just wide enough for the mule's, together with the rider's, feet. In many places the path is very treacherous and slippery, but, where the rut is deep enough to reach the underlying tufa, the road is excellent. In the river courses all the varieties of Chimborazo trachyte or andesite are exposed, many of which resemble, superficially, some that are to be seen on Isle St. Ignace and elsewhere on Lake Superior. At Chuquiboquio we come down to an elevation of 11,820 feet, and join the highway from Riobamba to Ambato, thirty feet wide, and paved in many places for long distances. It seems strange that so much labour should be expended in paving a road thirty feet wide upon which no carriages travel, and that the most difficult part of the pass over the Western Cordillera, from Panza to Chuquiboquio, should be left to be trodden out by the mules and their drivers. Towards Mocha a long stretch of the road is paved, probably in a difficult because level place, but fifteen feet would have been wide enough for a mule road. And further, as a mule road, it seems to be useless, for the mules will not use it unless compelled, and the muleteers allow their animals, in many places, to tread out new paths of the old sort by the side of the highway. Very often, too, the old pre-existing black ruts are travelled, and preferred to the new and dry but very hard causeway. The paving-stones used are all water-worn, and consist largely of greenstones. The newer volcanic rocks are rarely used, and seem to be too soft and prone to disintegrate.

By a long and very gradual descent we come down from the Cerro Ygualata to Mocha, 10,770 feet high, and then to Ambato, 8,550 feet, and so reach about the same level as Guaranda, on the Pacific side of the Western Cordillera. The afternoon spent on this part of the journey was cloudy and lowering, and although it did not rain it prevented our seeing the splendid mountain scenery surrounding the valley of the Ambato. But, on the way back, the weather was more favourable, and at a point about two miles north of Mocha I enjoyed the sight of the most beautiful panorama I had yet seen of Andean scenery. Northward, towards Ambato, that city is not itself observable, as it lies hidden in the depression occupied by the river of the same name. Beyond it rise minor eminences separating Ambato valley from the plain of Latacunga, the hills draining into which are plainly seen beyond it, covered with green pastures high up into the recesses of the Eastern Cordillera. Surmounting this chain, the snow at the base of Cotopaxi may be seen, but the beautiful cone of the volcano itself is hidden by the envious clouds which, at times, adhere most tenaciously to those high peaks. More to the east, the Cordillera rises higher than usual into the mountain Llanganati, and is more precipitous, especially towards Baños, where it is broken through by the deep glen which takes the River Pastassa to the Amazon. But, precipitous though the mountains are, the green patches climb up into the most foolhardy places. Southeastward the Cordillera is hidden by the Cerro Ygualata, but behind and towering over this range is seen the majestic peak of Tunguragua. Snow fills what seems to be a crater on its summit, and also the crevices on its sides. Further south than Tunguragua, the horns of the altar, or Capac Urcu, are seen projecting above the Cerro Ygualata, which occupies the southwestern part of our panorama, and rises in places to a height of 14,600 feet. West of Mocha the horizon is occupied by an isolated flat-topped mountain called Ponialica, 13,110 feet high, which has evidently yielded the numerous lava streams intersected by the road north of Mocha. The snow-clad crests of Chimborazo and Cari Cuirazo fill in the horizon to the southwest. No words of mine could possibly exaggerate the magnificence of this scenery,—and in proof of this I shall quote the words of another traveller, who viewed the same objects from a slightly different point of view. Reiss, in writing from Riobamba to Vom Rath, on the 6th April, 1874, quotes Schmarda's description, which says:—" The panorama " of Riobamba is the most magnificent, and perhaps the " most beautiful, upon the face of the earth. Three-" quarters of the horizon are occupied by extinct volcanoes, " now covered with glittering snow; in the west rises " Chimborazo like a gigantic silver bell, from which a " snow-covered ridge apparently leads to Cari Cuirazo; in " the northeast Tunguragua, clothed with forest at its " base, stretches up like a tower towards heaven, and " beside it stands the Altar of the Spaniards." Two objects in this panorama deserve more than a passing notice, namely, the volcanoes of Cotopaxi and Tunguragua; not because of any original observations of mine, but on account of the investigations which have recently been made into their mode of activity.

Apart from the earlier doubtful eruptions of Cotopaxi, said to have taken place about the time of the conquest of Peru by the Spaniards, its activity in historical times begins in 1742. With this year, after more than two centuries quiescence, it enters a stage of energetic wakefulness, lasting many years, and culminating, from time to time, in frightfully destructive eruptions. The phenomena attending these varied, of course, on each occasion, and among them may be noticed violent explosions, smoke and ash clouds above the crater, showers of stones, rapilli and ashes, overflows of lava, and fearful floods of water and mud, inundating or carrying away the towns and villages at the base of the mountain. The mention of lava streams may appear strange to many, for, since Humboldt's time, it has almost been received as an axiom that the volcanoes of Ecuador have not produced lava streams in historic periods, and certainly not discharged them from their summits, and that they have only yielded eruptions of mud. These mud and water floods were supposed to have been produced by the melting of the snow on the upper part of the cone, owing to its having been heated up, in fact generally warmed through by the subterranean heat beneath. The fact that, during eruptions, the snow on the summit apparently disappeared and the top of the mountain assumed the ordinary colour of earth and rock, seems to have given rise to this old view of the way in which Cotopaxi behaved. It is now understood, however, that no general melting off of the snow takes place, but that it is only covered up by the rapilli and ashes thrown out by the crater. It has further been ascertained that what the natives regarded as rents or cracks in the upper part of the cone during an eruption, were in reality red and glowing streams of melted lava stretching from the crater downwards. The lava of these streams, however, was never poured forth in such quantity as to enable them to reach the bottom of the mountain. They solidified mostly high up on its sides, and in localities seldom trodden by the foot of man. It was otherwise with the snow which these same lava streams displaced and melted. In some cases bands of snow and ice 6,000 feet long, thirty or forty feet thick, and perhaps a mile wide, must have been suddenly set at liberty in the form of a huge torrent, laden with volcanic debris of every description. Such a torrent, on the 9th December, 1742, swept away one-fourth of the town of Latacunga, the whole of the village of Rumibamba, and destroyed numerous mills, factories and haciendas, besides causing great loss of life. As late as the 14th September, 1853, from a similar cause, a rise took place in the Rio Cutuchi and caused the destruction of the bridge of Latacunga, twelve feet higher than the stream. Thrice on the samo day the river rose, carrying with it blocks from the lower end of the lava stream, which reached Latacunga in such a red-hot condition that easily-ignited materials were kindled when brought in contact with them. An old writer, named Velasco, in describing the eruption of 30th November, 1744, assumes that the water was ejected from the crater of the volcano, and mentions that it had formed a deep gutter from the crater downwards, over a league broad, which for several years afterwards remained free from snow. There is every reason for believing that this gutter was in reality the course of a lava stream, which remained for a long time hot enough to melt all the snow which fell on it. This is fully confirmed by the results of the information obtained and the observations made by Karsten, Reiss, and Stubel, regarding the eruption of 14th September, 1853. For many a month, Messrs. Reiss and Stubel wandered over the highest parts of Cotopaxi, and studied the details of its lava eruptions with the greatest care. Among others, they discovered the lava stream of 1853, and for four days investigated the manner of its occurrence. It appears to have flowed out of the crater, and rapidly down the steep part of the summit of the mountain, which has an inclination of 40°. Here none of the lava could remain, but the solidification and deposit began at a height of 5 500 metres (18,045 feet), and continued down to the snow-line, 4,600 metres (15,192 feet), where it formed a broad sea of lava. In 1872 this lava was still warm and free from snow, and, in fact, it was owing to this circumstance that Reiss was able to ascend to the very top of Cotopaxi, a height of 19,500 feet, through the regions of everlasting snow. His way lay upwards over the rough surface of the warm lava to a height of 4,600 metres (15,192 feet), and then over a thoroughly warmed sand bottom until the edge of the crater was nearly reached, when lava again afforded him a secure footing. The ascent by cutting steps into the steep ice covering would have been an undertaking altogether impossible, and the circumstances attending the scaling of the steep cone of Cotopaxi, by Dr. Reiss, afford us the best proof of the correctness of the views he advocates as to the *modus operandi* of this highest among volcanoes.

It is very worthy of remark that some of the eruptions of Tunguragua took place while Cotopaxi was enjoying a period of rest, namely, from the year 1768 until the beginning of the present century. In fact, it does not appear that any of the eruptions of those giant volcanoes took place simultaneously. Previous to the outbreak of Cotopaxi in 1742, the volcanic activity of Ecuador found a vent in the fearful eruptions and convulsions of Pichincha and the neighbourhood of the city of Quito. Dr. Stubel, of Mannheim, was the first geologist who ascended the peak of Tunguragua and found its elevation to be 5,087 metres, or 16,680 feet. This happened in February, 1873, when the crater was found to contain fumerolles in slight activity. Up till this time it was believed by scientific men that no overflow of lava had taken place from the crater, but that eruptions had burst out lower down on the sides of the mountain. It had also been maintained that the fresh-looking lava stream of Banjos had been erupted in the year 1777, not in a fused condition but in the solid state, by "a slow breaking through and building up of the " andesite blocks, accompanied by a terrible noise of " cracking and rock-rending." This is another of those indefinite, and therefore attractive, pictures which have been rudely torn to pieces by modern investigation. Dr. Stubel, in his letter to the President of the Republic, published in 1873, gives this report of the results of his observations :—" The lava outbreak of Pondo no doubt " took place on the declivity of the lower part of Tungura-" gua, but the last eruption, towards the end of last " century, and which yielded the Banjos lava, took place " out of the crater on the summit. It is true that at the " first glance one cannot convince himself of the fact, " because the cooled and solidified lava stream, as it lies " at present, does not begin at the edge of the crater. It " appears rather as if it had broken out half-way down the " mountain. But the circumstance that no continuity of " the lava stream is observable, from where it apparently " begins, up to the crater, is very easily explained and is " very natural. The inclination of this part of the moun-" tain is 35°, and the liquid lava must have shot rapidly " down over it, and all of it must have rolled down over " the pumice stone blocks and loose sand before it could " have solidified. When I ascended the crater, I found " hanging over a rock at its edge a huge mass of the same " lava which is now to be found damming across the Rio " Pastassa at Banjos." Other circumstances render the solid elevation theory impossible, and the fact that the lava rests upon chlorite and mica schists takes the foundation from the hypothesis altogether.

It seems, therefore, that the volcanic formations of South America, heretofore regarded as exceptional in character, are subjected to the same laws which have been observed to regulate similar outbreaks in Europe, although their immense extent and the surprising development of isolated peaks, rising high above the snow-line, surround them with phenomena to which volcanoes in Europe are entire strangers. The travellers to whose investigations we owe so much—Reiss of Dresden, and Stubel of Mannheim—arrived in South America in 1868, and only left it shortly before I visited Ambato in 1876, thus spending eight years in the most arduous and painstaking scientific work ever undertaken. This they have done entirely at their own cost, and their only reward will be the enhanced reputation which their labours will assuredly bring them, and the satisfaction they will experience from having done their duty in their particular sphere of life. It is to be regretted that so few among the monied people of this continent are to be found willing to fit out their sons mentally and materially for doing similar work.

While referring to new results in this field of volcanology, I cannot omit mentioning another, Dr. Theodore Wolf, of Guayaquil, whose labours in Ecuador have been equally as severe and fruitful as those of Reiss and Stubel. The result I refer to is the discovery of quartz in many of the recent volcanic rocks of the Andes. In the andesite of Puellaro, near the volcana Mojanda; in that of Achupallas, which belongs to the volcanic centre of Antisana, and in that of a locality to the south of Riobamba, quartz was observed and determined in large quantity,—and even in the lava of Pinantura, forming the largest stream yielded by the volcano Antisana, the same mineral was found as an essential constituent. Similar observations were made by David Forbes during his residence in Bolivia and Peru, and the fact can no longer be disputed that recent and historic lavas frequently contain quartz. One of the objections to the igneous origin of many granites is the presence of quartz, but this will surely cease to be regarded as a difficulty when it is found that recently erupted, undoubtedly igneous, lavas can produce it in cooling and solidifying.

The farthest point which I reached northeastward in my journey was the city of Ambato. It was built at the beginning of last century, the former place of the same name, and situated at a somewhat lower level, having been destroyed by an earthquake on the 25th June, 1698. The circumstances attending this earthquake were peculiar. At 1 o'clock in the morning the ground began to vibrate so fearfully that at the second shock not a house was left standing. Whole families were buried under the ruins of their houses, and those who were not killed in this way, and cried for help beneath the debris, were destroyed by another cause : for, about a quarter of an hour after the earthquake, a mud inundation overwhelmed the town, and every one engaged in rendering help fled to the hills. These floods came from the neighbourhood of Cari Cuairazo, whose summit is said to have fallen in and to have caused the discharge of water and mud from its interior. Wolf has shewn that nothing of this sort could possibly have happened, and is inclined to suppose that the bounds of some small lakes or lagoons must have been so disturbed by the earthquake as to permit their waters to break through and form the landslides and mud floods which were so destructive. This leads me to remark that one peculiarity of Andean scenery is the almost total absence of lakes.

During the whole of my ride I only saw one at a great distance off, and, judging from Villavicencio's map, they are of rare occurrence when compared, in this respect, with our northern countries. When it is considered that these mountains are generally covered with a large depth of alluvium, it becomes evident that many lakes formerly existing may have been discharged through the rents or loosened ground formed by the frequently occurring earthquakes.

IV.—ECUADOR.

"For the husband is the head of the wife, even as Christ is the head of the Church." Eph. v., 23.

The morning of the 19th May was beautifully bright, and I employed it very advantageously in strolling through the streets of Ambato. They are tolerably clean, intersect each other at right angles, and their buildings, mostly one-storied, of adobe blocks with tiled roofs, increase in respectability the closer their proximity to the Plaza. Passing an open window, I heard music from a piano, and wondered how the enterprising proprietor had been able to bring it so far inland. It was very much out of tune, which did not surprise me. The strains were an attempt at rendering, in some manner or other, the duet "Strahlt auf mich," from the Barber of Seville, which shews that the fine arts are cultivated even in Ambato. The Plaza is roomy and unobstructed, with, as usual, the church occupying one of its sides. The door was wide open, but facing it on entering was a large screen with a painting representing the woman taken in adultery. Stepping past, I found that mass was being celebrated. There was no musical accompaniment, but a plentiful bell-ringing to be heard, and about a dozen motionless female figures in kneeling posture to be seen. Here, as in Panama, Guayaquil and Lima, the men seem, for the most part, to take but little interest in attending to their religious "duty." And, after all, there would seem to be an appropriateness in the zeal and devotion displayed by the feminine portion of the human race all over the world in the service of their various churches. As the father, in the constitution of the family, corresponds to the State in national existence, so the mother plainly answers to the Church,—and both have their office and duty in training respectively the children and the people in good breeding, morality and vital religion. As the Church universal is the bride of Him who is King of kings and Lord of lords, so the visible Church in a civilized State ought to be a worthy helpmeet for the Government, and assist in so training the subject, and so impregnating him with good principles, as to cause him to yield a willing and intelligent obedience to the laws imposed by the State. This is, I believe, the correct theory, but its application is not to be found in the Republic of Ecuador.

Returned to the hotel, I breakfasted at the usual hour in these tropical countries, namely, 11 A.M., with the Columbian, who was quite disconsolate at our approaching separation. He despaired of finding, on his way to Quito and Popayan, any kind-hearted *Cristianos* to give him a lift on his journey as I had done. I have no doubt, however, that he soon found another *patron*. My quarters at the hotel in Ambato were the most comfortable I had yet occupied in Ecuador. They were very spacious as well; the sitting-room measured forty by twenty feet, with a bed-room at one end twenty by eight—both were roughly carpeted. The walls were massive to correspond, four feet thick and plastered and papered.

I had some lively bargaining, before setting out on my return journey to Guayaquil, with the muleteers as to the cost of two animals and peon back to Granada. Sixteen pesos were demanded for the service, and a bargain ultimately struck for eight—the same price I had paid on the way up. When it is considered that for this sum, about $6.40 Canadian currency, I had the services of a horse, a mule, and a peon for two days and a-half, and that quite possibly they might have to return to Ambato without hire, the price certainly does not appear exorbitant. But money is scarce in the interior of Ecuador, and a traveller is quite a godsend. Some of the natives looked at the coins, which I occasionally paid away, with a curiosity and intentness which plainly shewed that they were unaccustomed to the sight of money.

I left Ambato about one in the afternoon, following exactly the same route down as in ascending the Andes, but travelling more slowly in order to examine the rock exposures more closely and to collect rock specimens. This latter operation was thoroughly incomprehensible to my peon, and his disgust at my frequent stoppages was very evident. I found afterwards that I was described to other travellers, who were going in the same direction about that time, as the man who picked up stones. The ride from Ambato to Mocha I thoroughly enjoyed, being in full view of the magnificent scenery already described. About half-way I encountered my friend the Commandant, whom I had last seen at Guaranda. It seemed that he had been to me, on the ride up, as the hare to the tortoise in the fable. He was on his way to Quito, and, regretting that I was going back so soon, bade me heartily "A Dios." At Mocha, where I remained over night, I was followed round the village by a crowd of rather sceptical boys, who, nevertheless, very much admired my *martillito* (little hammer), which I used in obtaining specimens. A group of men, equally curious, afterwards invaded my quarters, which were very dark and dismal, and tried to study my map of Ecuador, which was evidently the first thing of the kind they had ever seen. But they were very persevering in the pursuit of knowledge under difficulties, and I only got rid of them

by writing silently and persistently. As for asking *them* for information, I had given up that idea after reading Dr. Wolf's testimony as to their reliability. " It is very diffi-
" cult," says he, "to obtain satisfactory information as
" regards the occurrences (earthquakes, &c.,) even of the
" past twenty years. The statements of so-called eyewit-
" nesses are entirely untrustworthy, and he who has ever
" in this country attempted to cross question such wit-
" nesses, well knows that one usually hears only lies or the
" most contradictory nonsense. It is useless to look for
" scientific interest or love of truth among modern Ecua-
" dorians." And the Government is a faithful reflex of the people. " It is a phenomenon characteristic of the South
" American republics that from the beginning of the
" eighteenth century, or the time of the continual civil
" wars, almost all sources of scientific information fail.
"While the old Spaniards considered it sufficiently impor-
" tant to hand down to their successors written descriptions
" of earthquakes and eruptions, the modern 'patriots' do
" not consider it worth the trouble to note these matters
" any further than perhaps in a newspaper, and then only
" superficially and incorrectly."*

Next morning I found that it had rained very heavily during the night, but it soon cleared up, and the weather offered no obstacle to my stone-picking. The basic lava streams between Mocha and Chuquibogio, as well as the benches of andesite higher up towards Chimborazo, were duly hammered at in spite of the peon's reluctance. But, in the presence of the huge mountains around, I felt very insignificant, and realised how futile the efforts and observations of even the best geologists may be in such an

*Geognostische Mittheilungen aus Ecuador, Neues Jahrbuch fur Mineralogie 1875; p. 67.

immense mountain region, and where both recent and ancient geographical changes have taken place on such a stupendous scale. I, at the same time, became fully aware of the justice of Scheerer's satire upon the geologists of his day. The late Prof. Scheerer, of Freiburg, in Saxony, was not only a distinguished chemist and geologist, but a true poet, as many of his prose writings testify. He wrote the satire in question in the *Fremdenbuch* of a hotel in the Fassa valley, Tirol. I have attempted, in the following lines, to render it into English :

> Full many a hundred thousand years ago,
> A mighty Traveller rode this valley through ;
> It was the world's Creator, and His wheels
> Left traces deep in Val di Fassa's hills.
> To-day there follow His career gigantic
> Crowds of professors, curious and pedantic ;
> Studying and tapping every rock and stone,
> And asking *them* about the times bygone.
> Where the great Traveller went, and how He sped?
> What was the meaning of the course He led?
> Why did He not confine the Fassa granite
> Within its orderly and proper limit?
> And how allow those fast young Dolomites
> To loosely flirt among the porphyrites?
> Many a hero splits his head in thinking,
> And soon opines he's got the thing like winking ;
> But yet, I fear, that what for truth he holds,
> Is but a cloak of learning with vain folds.
> He who believes he knows how wrought the Master,
> Knows but the whims his head produces faster.
> He who on rocks and stones doth try a race,[*]
> Is surely on a useless wild goose chase.

Late in the afternoon, a little below Tortorillas, I was fortunate enough to meet a herd of llamas, of which I had previously seen only single specimens. They were all loaded, although not too heavily, and, in passing, they

---

[*] The last two lines do not exactly carry the meaning of the original, which is as follows :

> Wer auf dem weg des steins sich brustet voller stolzes
> Befindet sich nicht selten auf dem weg des Holzes.

scanned me with their large bright eyes quite enquiringly. They are of a dark-brown colour, exactly resembling, round the head and neck, that of Jersey cattle, while in shape they have a distant resemblance to diminutive camels. It may be for this reason, as well as on account of their use as beasts of burden, that they have been named the "camels of the Andes." It was dusk when I reached Tortorillas, where I had to spend the night, although more comfortable than on the former occasion. I indulged, to the utmost of my ability, in conversation with the muleteers who were also staying over at this place. They were employed carrying potatoes from Ambato to Bodegas, where they were sold at five pesos per mule-load—or about eighty cents per bushel. I pitied these poor agriculturists, who have thus to travel four days over the ridge of the Western Cordillera, and sell their goods at a price which scarcely pays for their own time and that of the animals. It is as if the farmers around Kingston were to bring their produce on horseback to Montreal, and sell it there at market prices. But to such straits the inhabitants of a purely agricultural country are frequently reduced. The muleteers, although outwardly polite towards me, were, I fear, inwardly contemptuous, for I heard them afterwards, when they imagined me to be asleep, sneering at and mimicing my imperfect Spanish.

After leaving Tortorillas early next day (21st May) and again reaching the highest point on the route over the Western Cordilleras, the weather became quite clear and bright, and I obtained from the "Arenal" another unobstructed view of the southern and western aspects of Chimborazo. But still, a layer of pure white cloud clung to the upper part of the dome, and this although a strong easterly wind prevailed. Perhaps this vapour was the result of the condensation, by the icy atmosphere around Chimborazo, of the moisture brought by the east wind from the humid valleys of Brazil. The mountain is very rugged at the base of the dome, and immense ridges of rock break through the snow-covering and project far out on to the Cordillera. From the hut, Panza, down to the bottom of the first *quebrada*, a distance in vertical height of about 4,000 feet, the rock exposures are very numerous, and not at all volcanic in character. I could not avoid again remarking their resemblance to the massive and schistose greenstones which characterize the Huronian system in Northwestern Ontario. It would thus seem that these ancient rocks extend up to a height of 13,000 feet on the west side of the Western Cordillera, and that the fused products of volcanic activity found a vent chiefly on its eastern side, while the fragmentary ejections of the elevated cones were scattered around on all sides. In the bed of the first river crossed after descending from the pass, fragments of coarse conglomerate are to be seen which I had not observed *in situ* higher up.

In riding across the wearisome though picturesque *quebradas* which intersect the road from the base of the Cordillera to Guaranda, and in passing along the road to the latter place, I seemed to encounter an unusually large number of passengers of every description. I mention first those to whose appearance I had become accustomed. Toiling along on foot came the poor Indian women, heavily burdened even when their male companions have comparatively little on their shoulders. It is to be noticed that this work brings out a high, almost crimson, colour on the swarthy cheeks of the women. No mule or llama have they to carry their burdens for them, far less whereon they may rest their weary limbs. Their salutation is uttered sometimes in their own Indian or Quechua language, but more frequently in Spanish, and they vary it very conscientiously according to the time of day. *Buenas dias, buena tarde*, and *buena noche* are used respectively for the morning, afternoon and evening. Somewhat higher in the social scale probably than these, but still unmounted, comes the muleteer, with bare feet, tough and hardened, striding along behind a train of animals, always urging them onward by cracking his whip or uttering not very choice expressions. He is not at all so polite or so particular in his greeting as the Indians, and in meeting an evident foreigner is sometimes altogether silent. This is sure to be the case if he happen to have mounted one of his mules. Of the better class of the population, always mounted on small active horses, and well-furnished as regards *montura*, I met an unusually large number in the course of the afternoon,—but it was not until several of these horsemen had attempted conversation with me that I began to understand that something unusual was on foot. I was asked whether I had seen a certain Gen. Veintemiljas (Gen. Twentymiles), and whether I knew when he had left Ambato or reached Tortorillas. These questions were asked me not once but twenty times, and I subsequently understood that this general was on his way to Guayaquil to replace the "Commandant" whose acquaintance I had made in ascending the Andes. The General appeared to be a distinguished ornament of the Republic, for, on coming within a few miles of Guaranda, I passed a large group of horsemen, not in uniform but drawn up in line to receive him. Nearer to the town, little knots of horsemen and long strings of Indians on foot were passed. One of these had fallen a victim to the influence of *aguardiente* (fire-water), and lay helplessly drunk at the roadside.

His faithful better-half, together with a mule and *carga*, were waiting beside him patiently and philosophically for his recovery.

On reaching Guaranda, I fully realised that it was a gala day, although a Sunday. A band of music struck up as I descended the hill overlooking the town, and the movements of my horse shewed plainly that he was unaccustomed to such demonstrations. My greatest fear was that of being mistaken for the General, and I was quite thankful to reach the hotel without mishap. Here I was duly welcomed by Mephistopheles, and quartered in a room overlooking the Plaza. At supper I made the acquaintance of a German merchant from Guayaquil, and after having been in a manner tongue-tied (at least to Spanish) I fear I became very garrulous both in German and English. We adjourned to the balcony of the hotel, overlooking the Plaza, and discussed the whole Republic, from the top of Chimborazo to the level of the Pacific. Herr Weinberg was disconsolate about the state of business; never before had it been so dull or cash so scarce. Superadded to these troubles came others of a private and personal nature. He had been harshly treated by some of the natives, and was at war with them. They were half-civilized robbers, fitted only to be ruled by an iron, despotic hand. I suggested that Kaiser Wilhelm ought to subdue Ecuador and convert it into a German colony, but Herr Weinberg claimed to be a Russian, and did not quite approve of the proposal.

Our philosophizing was interrupted by a burst of brass music and the arrival on the Plaza of Gen. Twentymiles, with all the horsemen in his train whom I had passed during the afternoon. There followed him, besides, "round the square," a troop of footsoldiers of the most heterogeneous description. A review of these afterwards took place in the Plaza, evidently in honour of the General; but he was not present, which shewed his great good sense. It would have required superhuman courage, or impudence, to have faced, or rather countenanced, such troops. In numbers there might have been a regiment present, but they were minus "regimentals." Or rather these were exhibited in refreshing variety. One man wore a blue coat and brass buttons, while another was in his shirtsleeves; one soldier had shoes, his comrade none. In one particular only they agreed; all had trousers of some description, either dark, white or bed-tick pattern. They were evidently discouraged at the absence of the General, for they took themselves and their music off after about fifteen minutes drill. In complexion, dark features certainly prevailed among these men,—and I began to understand that the unquiet people who supported *pronunciamientos* and effected revolutions were not the natives of the rural and mountain districts, but the negroes and half-breeds of the towns and seaports. After dark the General was serenaded by a brass band which discoursed some really beautiful music, mostly operatic overtures and fantasias, until 11 o'clock, about which time I "turned in." Tired as I was, I could not help commiserating the poor Republic of Ecuador; a sovereign State at the mercy of such a rabble as I had seen on the Plaza; a father, whose children treat him with contempt and violence on the slightest pretext, and yet look to him for the means to enable them to lead a thriftless, indolent life. For, it is said to be a fact, that nowhere is such a large proportion of the population employed by the State as in Ecuador and Peru. The revolutions in these countries may be compared to "strikes," the object, however, being not so much increase of wages as universal employment by the State.

The 22nd May opened with a beautifully bright morning, and I said good-bye to Mephistopheles and Guaranda very willingly. Nothing of interest happened on the way to Chapacota, which place we passed through about noon. Very few inhabitants were visible in the streets; a few sat knitting or spinning on their doorsteps, and a couple of men were seen building an adobe fence. The blocks which it consisted of are moulded *in situ*, in bottomless boxes, the sides and ends of which are afterwards removed. Most of the village population seemed to be in the fields, and in passing these I sometimes observed a whole family at work picking out weeds from among the young grain. In one pasture, I observed an old woman herding sheep and spinning with the distaff at the same time. From all this I drew the conclusion that the rural inhabitants of Ecuador, although quite unintelligent, are contented and industrious, and that, if Inca civilization has left such traces after centuries of Spanish misrule, Prescott's description of it could not have been much exaggerated.

The sun was low in the sky when I reached the heights above Puzo, and scrambled along and down their miry and slippery mule-paths. My horse frequently slid down these on his haunches, and I had at last to dismount and lead him down after me until I reached the new road. There the zigzagging in the mountain sides began, and the orb of day sank down behind the foothills in the west. The sun is very business-like and unpoetic in these equatorial regions. He bolts up quite hurriedly and perpendicularly in the morning, climbs over our heads so that it is rather troublesome to find his whereabouts, and then plunges down in the west almost without giving us time to say good-bye, and without troubling the clouds to be in attendance. He is quite a different being in the north, where his gradual rise and slanting descent affords the observer abundant time to notice his progress and the beauty of the surrounding heavens. The contrast is striking, and reminded me of some lines I had written years ago in Norway in praise of northern summer evenings, and which may here be introduced:

  When wintry snows in floods have gone,
   And biting frosts are fled,
  When quickly green the fields have grown,
   And trees their bloom outspread,
  When deep the cuckoo chants her cry
   Amongst closely crowding leaves,
  What time and circumstance can vie
   With northern summer eves?

  The hills so late with snow and pine
   Antagonistic dressed,
  Now clothed anew resplendent shine
   From corn-clad base to crest
  How glossy green that velvet train
   That birchen forest weaves
  O'er valley deep and mountain chain
   On northern summer eves.

  The envious clouds that all the day
   Like cowards fled the sun,
  Now gath'ring wary, track his way
   When all his strength is gone.
  The long and sword-like gilded clouds
   The world of light bereave,
  And rosy-tinged are lake and wood
   By northern sun and eve.

  Jehovah's world is beautiful,
   His household well maintained,—
  How patient, good and dutiful
   His children are uptrained?
  How blest the man who as such scenes
   He calm and thoughtful leaves,
  Can guide his footseps by the light
   Of northern summer eves.

It became quite dark long before we reached Puzo, and in passing along the unfenced road I found my safety in keeping within sight of the wall side of the notched out road. and leaving the precipices on the other as far off as possible. When we arrived at Puzo everything was dark, the *patrona* asleep, and the verandah encumbered with drowsy peons crouched among their *cargas*. But the *patrona* was soon roused, and willingly prepared us supper, after which I scrambled up to the flat above, and was soon sound asleep.

My journey of next day (23rd May) was down over the next to impassable road from Palsabamba to Playas, described in last chapter. At Playas I recollected the address given me at Puzo in ascending the mountains by the Commandant, and enquired persistently for the residence of Señor Pablo Hurtado. I was directed to a large roomy building, evidently bolonging to a cocoa plantation, and here I found the Señor in his counting-house employed in settling with some of his hands for their work. I recognised him as one of the passengers with whom I had travelled on board the " Quito " from Guayaquil to Bodegas. He was very friendly and hospitable, and very talkative, and made not the slightest allowance for my inexperience in the language. He was very severe on his workmen, blamed their laziness, and denounced the plantain tree as the ruin of the country. With a few of these in his garden, requiring scarcely any attention, the negro can live without work, and only shews himself on the plantation when it pleases himself. His favourite occupation is swinging in a *hamac* and smoking, while his wife does any little work that is necessary in the garden. The Señor seemed very anxious to impress me favourably with a scheme of his for a new road from the head of navigable water, at a place called Tundulundun, to the mountains. The name of the starting point struck me as very curious, but I had the greatest difficulty in simulating interest in his scheme. At last supper was announced, which was rather a strange *melange*. First came the inevitable caldo or potato soup; afterwards a sort of omelette, and lastly a hot decoction in which milk, eggs and sugar were whipped up together to the consistence of thin porridge. Señor Hurtado was a planter, worked in fact several plantations, but his wife and family were, I understood, in Guayaquil. Nevertheless, I noticed a woman and children in quite close proximity to his apartments. But in Dibdin's old song, William complains to Black-eyed Susan of the landmen—

" They'll tell thee sailors when away
In ev'ry port a mistress find."

And, similarly, Ecuadorian planters might complain of misrepresentation, for I have heard that some of them are accused of having a family on each plantation.

I passed the night lying on the floor, tormented by mosquitoes, and next morning, the 24th, took leave of the planter, after having drank coffee with him and paid for my entertainment. I had now fairly returned again to the Guayaquil deepland, and the road, although level, was bottomless. From Playas to Palmar I followed the road *via* Savaneta, a different route from the one pursued when going eastward. For long distances the road had a small stream or ditch in its centre, and where the ground was sandy the animals preferred wading in the stream. But where the sand changed to clay ground and the bottom became deep and treacherous, they selected the mud corduroy of the road at the side.

I did not delay at Savaneta, where the inhabitants are negroes, and either lazy or uncivil. Indians from the mountains are not to be found resident in the deepland, the climate being quite fatal to them. Hence it is that in cultivating the plantations, dependance has to be placed solely on the negroes. The road onward to Palmar was slightly better, and here we crossed the Babahoyo and rejoined the road to Bodegas, which I recognised as having travelled on the 14th May when I avoided Savaneta altogether.

Early in the afternoon I reached Bodegas heartily tired of my ride of eleven days, and glad at the prospect of soon being able to leave Ecuador altogether. I knew that the "Truxillo" was to leave for Panama on the 26th, and was confident of being able to reach Guayaquil in time for her. After selling my *montura*, for which I had no further use,—and questioning several storekeepers as to the probable hours of sailing of the erratic river steamboats, I strolled along the street fronting the river in search of a café, for I felt quite ready for dinner. Turning into what appeared to be one, welcome English voices met my ear, and I luckily stumbled upon two Englishmen, Linwood and Carpenter, the latter an acquaintance from Guayaquil. My tongue immediately got full swing again for the second time in eleven days, and I felt disposed to empty out my whole mind to my new companions. But much as I was disposed to talk, I soon found that I was no match for my Guayaquil friend, who rattled on incessantly on all possible subjects. He and his companions were in search of orchid plants for export to Europe, and proposed to ascend the Caracol river and explore for them in the humid, luxurious forests along its banks.

"How did you find the road to the mountains?" asked Carpenter, after exhausting a few other subjects.

"For the first two days I could not find any roads," I replied.

"I suppose not—only mud and misery; but in the "mountains they are improving."

"No doubt," said I; "but some of the outlay there might "have been spared, and better expended down here."

"Perhaps; but you must remember that it is not more "than ten years since the whole road to Quito was in the "same condition as that between Bodegas and Palsabamba."

"Yes," added Linwood, "and if they had not killed "Garcia Moreno, by this time probably the whole would "have been finished."

"Was it he who began to improve the roads?" I enquired.

"Certainly it was," said Linwood. "Moreover, he was "energetic, patriotic and honest, although no doubt under "Jesuit influence."

"How did that shew itself?"

"He imported Jesuits from Europe to superintend cer-"tain educational institutions, and favoured them in many "ways, while he ruled the natives with a rod of iron."

"How do the Jesuits stand, as compared with the native "priesthood, in morals and culture?" I asked.

"I believe the Jesuits are incomparably superior," answered Linwood; "they are said to be far more "talented, and lead a godly life."

"And the priests?"

"Do you see that balsa?" asked Linwood, pointing from the window of the café to a hut floating on a raft, and moored to the bank of the river; "there lives the curé of "this parish with two women, his mistresses."

"But do you mean to say that that is a common thing?"

"It is too common to attract much attention."

From this and a good deal of other conversation it became apparent to me that the Jesuits in the *Roman Catholic Church* of Ecuador occupied a somewhat similar position to the Ritualists in the Anglican Church. It seems that the Jesuits were really sincere, earnest men, bent on saving the country and reforming the church in their particular fashion, and that Garcia Moreno had been of the same thorough character. A friend of mine, an Irishman, once said to me, after the assassination of McGee, in Montreal, with great bitterness : " It is only the Irish who kill their " best men." He was mistaken ; the American Turks are equally ungrateful. At the same time it must be said that the Jesuit plan of reformation in Ecuador does not appear by any means to have been correct in principle. Garcia Moreno, Dictator, who might have said, like Louis XIV., " The state ! I am the state," was subject, and allowed himself to be subject, to the church as represented by the Society of Jesus. The Jesuits fully assumed the supremacy of the church over the state, and busied themselves more about state business than about the moral training of the people. But, perhaps, their sway was not sufficiently long continued to enable them to gain complete control of educational matters. In any case they put the church into the position of a wife who exhibits more desire to rule her husband than to care for his children, and who is more occupied with ceremony and fashion than with useful domestic affairs.

On the morning of the 25th May the " Quito " arrived from Caracol, and it was announced that she would leave for Guayaquil at noon. After getting myself and baggage on board at that time, I found that her departure was postponed until next morning, in order that General Twentymiles, who had just arrived in Bodegas, might be accommodated. I expostulated with the captain, telling him that I would be sure to miss the "Truxillo" at Guayaquil if he waited till next morning. He laid the blame on the General, and I made bold enough to wait on the great man himself and explain my case. He received me very graciously, conversed in French, and promised that he would speak to the captain and try to accelerate his departure. But nothing was changed in their arrangements, and I found that in a free (?) republic in South America, a general, or the captain of an insignificant steamboat could arbitrarily detain the public conveyances in a manner which even Queen Victoria would not permit herself to do in England.

The "Quito" did not leave Bodegas until next morning about six o'clock, by which hour Gen. Twentymiles and staff came on board. Among the passengers was a Mr. Wilson, civil engineer, of Guayaquil, who had spent over twelve years in Ecuador, and from whom I derived a great deal of information. He was extremely well versed in ethnology, and had evidently studied with much care the origin of the South American Indians. This is of course a part of the much larger question as to the manner in which the American continent was peopled. Mr. Wilson maintained that the aborigines of South America had an independant origin, were *original* in fact, and combated the idea that their predecessors could ever have been derived from Asia. He considered it much more likely that the Asiatic continent had been peopled from America than that the contrary process took place, and maintained that the currents of the Pacific, which always flowed westward, were instrumental in effecting the operation. To me it seemed quite as likely that the original peoplers of this continent may have come from the west, feeling their way little by little via the Aleutian Islands, or Behrings Straits.

The day passed very quickly and the "Quito" arrived at Guayaquil early in the afternoon, but the "Truxillo" had left in the morning. There was a great turn out here also to meet the general, who stood beside the captain and bowed to the populace like an actor called before the curtain. I afterwards learned than an incipient insurrection had been discovered in Guayaquil, and that the change of "commandants" had been in some way or other connected with it. Armstrong was waiting my arrival at the wharf, and we adjourned to the "Hotel de nueve Octobre" —the Ninth of October Hotel—where we proposed to wait till the 1st June for the next steamer.

This stay of six days in Guayaquil enabled me to widen my experiences very much as regards that city. The hotel consisted of a series of rooms on the second story, none of which were blessed with windows, and the light to which in the daytime was always introduced by the open door. My room door opened towards the street fronting the river, and the view from it was always pleasant and lively. The furniture was rough and the beds hard, but still my quarters were infinitely preferable to those I had occupied at Playas and Tortorillas. Meals were procured at a café in the same street, and consisted of coffee at 8.00 A.M., breakfast at 11.00 A.M., and dinner at 4.00 in the afternoon. This arrangement resolved itself into two meals daily, quite enough certainly in a temperature of $80°$ or $85°$. The heat caused an extensive consumption of ice water and lemonade, in the use of which beverages I was, I fear, very intemperate. The natives do not seem to be contented with these however, judging from the number of signboards bearing the name "majorca," a sort of whiskey distilled from fermented syrup. The population in the streets consists mainly of negroes and mulattoes, with every gradation of dark line. Then came the cholados or half-bred, betwixt the European and native. There is very little pure Indian in the lowlands of Ecuador. All are Roman Catholic, but I fear bring little credit to that church. Besides the ordinary clergy there are frequently seen on the streets the Dominican in his white flannel; Franciscans in grey and closely shaven, as well as Capuchins in brown and well bearded. The buildings fronting the river are respectable and orderly. They are mostly three stories high, and each higher story has commonly the knack of projecting a little further into the street than the one immediately below it. Thus the second floor is frequently built out over the sidewalk and supported by columns, making it very agreeable for foot-passengers, protecting them from rain and storm. It is to be remarked that there is scarcely any other kind of passengers in Guayaquil than foot-passengers, for the simple reason that there are no vehicles, no carriages, carts or even wheelbarrows. The goods imported are taken from the wharves to the wholesale warehouses on trollies or platform cars running on an iron track, and single bales or packages of large size are borne on the shoulders of negroes or cholados. There are no private carriages, but there is one line of street cars running about two miles out to a bathing resort. Thus we have the strange sight of a railway track being introduced before the use of carts or wheelbarrows, and street cars before carriages. A walk out of the town at once furnishes the reason of all this. The streets degenerate into wide rutless tracks, and these again into mule paths or footpaths. But roads there are none; therefore wheels are useless. Outside of the town the mule, as we have seen, does the work of the railway car carriage and wheelbarrow, and this state of things continues until the traveller reaches the central valleys of the Andes.

Guayaquil from the river, thanks to plaster and whitewash, looks rather cleanly, but it is in reality a whited sepulchre. There is no system of sewerage nor array of scavengers, and the greatest possible neglect of cleanliness and decency. The Guayaquil city fathers in their sanitary endeavours seem to depend solely upon the crowds of condors, which feed upon the garbage of the streets, and upon the heavy down-pourings of the rainy season. The resulting state of things may be imagined but not described, and the exterior consequence is that with the name Guayaquil is associated the ideas of the infections and fevers which make it the abhorrence of all Europeans. Many worthy men believe that no cities can be worse in sanitary respects than Liverpool and Montreal. I think they would change their opinion if they visited Guayaquil and Panama. In this particular we again find the state cutting a very sorry figure. Cleanliness being next to godliness, it might be supposed that the church would interest herself on the subject. But, in most countries, the state through its various municipalities has taken charge of the public cleanlinesss and health. In Ecuador, however, the state resembles the father of a family who has not authority enough among his children to make them keep their faces and hands clean. Nor has the state vigour enough to stimulate industry in such a manner as to furnish the people with employment. In this respect Ecuador stands at the other extreme from the United States. While, in the latter country, the state is far too much absorbed in its own particular business; in Ecuador it commits the even greater mistake of neglecting altogether to attend to the material wants of the population. Hence it comes that the land is tilled with a wooden plough, and that potatoes are packed on mule-back over the Andes to find a market.

I frequently waited on Dr. Wolf after my return, and exchanged ideas with him regarding my observations in the mountains. I also obtained from him a great deal of information regarding the geology of Ecuador, and copies of some of his papers on the subject. From these I may here attempt to give a sketch of what is known regarding the geological architecture of the Andes. Beginning with the upper story, I translate from Wolf's description. If we consider the geological build of the highlands of Ecuador we may well maintain that the historic occurrences of a volcanic character, however fearful they appear to have been, are nevertheless only weak echoes from earlier epochs. The mountains of lava, and the incredible masses of volcanic tuff, rapilli, pumice stone, ashes, etc., which cover the surface of Upper Ecuador are the results of colossal and oft repeated outbreaks. As regards many of the greatest volcanoes, for instance, Cayambi, Colocachi, Corazon, Ilinisa, Chimborazo, etc., there exist no traditions concerning eruptions in connection with them, and yet there is no doubt that they, like the active volcanoes, were built up in the course of thousands of years by the action of the same forces. In no other part of the world have eruptive masses attained to such an enormous development and thickness as in Ecuador; but yet the oldest works of the human race, the oldest ruins of the Incas, have been erected upon volcanic debris, and are partly built up of recent lavas, so that we have good reason for concluding that no human being was witness to the principal volcanic outbreaks. The deep masses of tuff in the valley of Tumbaco and Chillo, those of the Province of Imbabura, those of the plain of

Riobamba, and at the base of Chimborazo, contain fossil bones of animals which enable us to determine, geologically, the time of their formation. According to these, they belong to the quaternary or post pliocene period, in which time certain mammals, now extinct, peopled these highlands. The remains of most frequent occurrence are those of *Mastodon Andium, Humb., Equus Quitensis, Cervus Chimborassi, Cervus Riobambensis,* and *Dasypus Magnus.* The last four of these are the names of new species, the descriptions of which, by Wolf, are now ready for publication. Among these, the horse is especially interesting, as it corresponds to no other living or fossil species. It is smaller, but more plump and robust in all its parts than *Equus Caballus,* and is found in almost every part of the highland of Quito.* In some places, and especially at a point near Riobamba, it occurs along with bones of the *mastodon.* This point is the Gorge of Chalang, near Punin, where the fossiliferous tuff rests directly on non-volcanic rocks, sandstone, quartzite, and siliceous conglomerate. Here the fossil remains of the extinct animals are mixed with those of species still existing. Since the fossiliferous tuff is the oldest in this region, it follows that the activity of the volcanoes of Ecuador is comparatively recent, and later than the Tertiary formation. The discovery of the bones of the horse decides an old disputed question among European palæontologists, namely, as to whether, in ancient times, the horse existed on South American territory. We know now that the horse lived among the Andes simultaneously with the mastodon, but that it had become extinct long before the conquest, since the Indians had never before seen anything like the horses

---

* Neues Jahrbuch fur Mineralogie, 1875.

of their conquerors. Thus it has been the strange fate of the horse to inhabit the South American continent at two very different periods; first, free and unfettered, among mountains as yet non-volcanic; and, secondly, under the harsh dominion of man.* At Chalang, Dr. Wolf excavated a skeleton of the horse almost complete, a proof that the bones still lie in their original place of deposit. *Cervus Chimborassi* is a true giant deer, exceeding in size the European *Cervus Hibernicus*, while *Cervus Riobambensis* resembles the modern Paramo deer, *Cervus Antisanensis*.

However enormously developed the eruptive rocks and volcanic products may be, they seem nevertheless only to constitute the attics and roof of the huge structure of the Andes. At lower levels there are found other rocks in great variety—such as granite, gneiss, crystalline schists, dark-coloured slates, greenstones, and greenstone schists, porphyries, Devonian carboniferous and Cretaceous strata.

As regards the geological constitution of the province of Guayaquil, and generally of that part of Ecuador lying between the Andes and the Pacific, there would seem to exist in this region, according to Dr. Wolf's investigations, five different formations: four sedimentary and one eruptive. The oldest is the Cretaceous formation, which forms the principal mountains of the province, lying between the Guayaquil Valley and the Pacific. The small hills near Guayaquil, and those which rise, island like, out of the alluvial plains of the rivers Daule and Bodegas, belong to the same formation, and are doubtless but the remains, which have escaped denudation, of much more extensive strata. The rocks are principally limestones, siliceous limestone, quartzite, silicic schist, and glaucomitic sand-

---

* Zeitschrift der Deutschen geologischen Gesellschaft, xxiv; p. 58.

stone, all inter-stratified with each other in their layers. The fossils are very scarce; but *Inoceramus flicatus* d'Orbigny, and *I. Roemeri* Karsten, have been discovered and determined.

The Cretaceous strata are, in many places, intersected by greenstones which also rise in isolated masses from the alluvial plain of the Guayaquil Valley. These greenstones are for the most part fine-grained diorites and entirely destitute of any schistose texture.

The quaternary formation is principally developed in the Island of Puna, the peninsular of Santa Elena, and along the Pacific Coast. Its rocks are for the most part horizontal sandstones, in which marine organisms occur mostly belonging to living species; but besides the remains of Mastodon Andium, Humb. have been found at Santa Elena. These occur in their original place of deposit, for all the foot-bones have frequently been found together in natural connection.

Unconformably overlaid at several points on the coast by these quaternary strata there are found beds of sandstones on edge, with which are intercalated seams of clay frequently bituminous. Fossils have not yet been discovered in them, but Dr. Wolf is inclined to regard them as of tertiary age. They may possibly also be the source of the petroleum which occurs at several places on the coast.

Besides these marine strata there is to be mentioned the youngest and quite modern fluviatile and fluvio-marine formation, which is still a process of deposition. This is the alluvial plain which is intersected by the Guayaquil River and its complicated net of tributaries and canals, and is as much a product of their activity as Lower Egypt has been of the Nile. It is easy to distinguish the fertile alluvium from the sandy and sterile quaternary formations. The former never rises very high above the level of the rivers, and only a couple of metres above that of the sea, and is for the most part inundated during the rainy season. It is this recent formation that is practically the most important because it is by far the most fruitful soil. The Cretaceous formation is only sparingly cultivated, and usually lightly covered with wooding, which loses its foliage periodically in summer. The sandy and saliferous quaternary region is incapable of cultivation, and presents in its almost desert-like character a striking contrast to the rest of Ecuador. On the other hand, the alluvial formation constitutes the source of the riches of the Province of Guayaquil. All the villages of any consequence, and the beautiful haciendas, which cause the river banks to appear like a continuous garden, are found on this deep alluvium.

How and in what manner the quaternary, tertiary and cretaceous strata of the Guayaquil deepland are connected with the volcanic highlands is a difficult problem which will probably remain a long time unsolved, because almost the whole region where the transition takes place, that is to say, the base and the slopes of the Andes are covered with the thickest and most impenetratable forest. Then on the few miserable roads which conduct through this forest, towards the Cordillera, the rocks are much concealed and only visible at their weathered and decomposed outcrops. It is impossible to obtain a clear idea of the position of the non-fossiliferous sandstones and slates which crop out in isolated localities far distant from each other. One thing is certain, that almost every where massive, schistose and slaty greenstones are to be observed. But cretaceous strata have been detected with characteristic fossils, very high up on the western declivity of the mountain Corazon, and immediately overlaid by volcanic material. Many an arduous excursion in the inhospitable Paramos, and into the out of the way uninhabited forests will yet require to be made before the geological structure of the Western Cordillera is explained, and our fragmentary knowledge concerning it is combined to a satisfactory whole. As regards the eastern slope of the Eastern Cordillera, which descends to the valleys and plains of the Amazon, far greater difficulties there beset the study of its geology, difficulties that are altogether insurmountable. To judge from the boulders in some of the river beds old crystalline schists seem to prevail. As far as observation goes, such rocks seem also to underlie the volcanic formations of Cayambi, Antisana, Cotopaxi and Tunguragua in the Eastern Cordillera. But of the geological structure of the eastern lowlands of Ecuador, and of the mountains which intersect them, we know simply nothing * Millions of square miles of mountain ridge and deep valley are spread out in South America awaiting the attention of future generations of geologists. And this wide expanse is simply a figure of the state of things existing not only in geology but in every other science. The amount of work to be done and the fields of investigation ever opening up are boundless, and each labourer, in his little life, can only accomplish any creditable work by confining himself to one little department of one particular science. In our inward lives, although it is our duty as Christians to strive ever towards something better and higher, we well know that perfection is unattainable. And so it is with our knowledge. Never, however much puny men may travel, and observe, discuss, and theorise,

---

* Neues Iahrbuch fur Mineralogie 1874.

will the immense theatre even of the physical world be fully investigated. At the end of the labours of unborn ages they will have to exclaim then as we must now : " O the " depth of the riches both of the wisdom and knowledge of " God! How unsearchable are his judgments, and his " ways past finding out."

While conversing with Dr. Wolf, it appeared to me that he was enthusiastically devoted to his science ; but he did not speak very confidently as to his future in the Republic. He seemed to think that its present authorities might put an end to his labours very summarily ; not, indeed, by dispensing with his services, but by forgetting to provide his salary. Although the former predominating Jesuit influence no longer exists, it appears that the present government have not by any means got their house in order, and that frequently the pay to their officials has run behind, leaving some of them at last in the position that they could neither live nor leave the country. The people who seem most sure of their remuneration are the priests, who are derived from the ranks of the common people, and have even special inducements held out to them to study for the church. In character and attainments they do not stand high : "They are not even theologians, far less cultivated " men," said one of my informants. Yet the state provides a university and many advantages for them. It is a pity that it does not go a step further, and provide some definite rational work for them, and make their pay depend on its proper performance. The church is a very expensive item in these republics ; but if it occupied its proper place it would only be furnished with a living by the state such as a good husband provides his wife. It, being bound to the state as to its earthly lord and master, should not be allowed to hold property, or acquire wealth. That should be all vested in the state, and dealt out to its "better-half," if at all, in conformity with the provisions of a well authenticated marriage contract. Then, of course, it would also require to be seen that the conditions binding upon the church should be fulfilled to the letter, and that it should not be allowed to be false or treasonable to the state without sacrificing position and emoluments. This matter of church and state connection would require ventilation in a good many countries, besides those of South America, before such a state of things is inaugurated as will be in itself just and right to both parties. But the world is in a fair way to see the disadvantage of misunderstanding this matter, and will soon wake up to see the necessity for some active positive policy to take the place of the drifting principle which now prevails. It is for us to remember that the state can also claim a divine origin: "for the ruler "beareth not the sword in vain, for he is the minister of "God."

There are probably not more than half a dozen English residents in Guayaquil, and their position is not to be envied. They are not very prosperous or powerful, and consequently do not receive very much consideration from the native authorities. But Armstrong and I nevertheless spent a good many pleasant hours in their company discussing British and South American affairs, as well as matters of church and state, trade and commerce, literature and art, very freely. One thing these isolated British subjects possess in common with the Canadians of the north, namely, intense affection of the mother land, pride in her strength and fame, and enthusiasm for the spread of her power and influence. So much was this the case that they enquired particularly about the British of North America, and their leanings and sentiments both as to annexation and confederation. I was able to answer their questions satisfactorily, and from colonial the subject of our conversation advanced to imperial federation with its difficulties and anticipated advantages. No doubt if that important matter had been left to us, we could have settled it in a manner satisfactory to all parties. We poor enthusiasts saw no difficulty in the way of introducing a uniform system of coinage, weights and measures, postages, and even of naval and military defence, for the whole of the British Dominions. Nor did we deem a *Zoliverein* of Great Britain with all her colonies, dependencies and possessions, such an impracticable affair. When, however, we reached taxation, parliamentary representation, etc., we became rather undecided, and at last agreed to postpone the conference. One of our English acquaintances in Guayaquil was a photographer, and kindly furnished me with some of the views which he had taken in the town and vicinity.

When the matter is well considered it appears strange that there should be such a small number of English-speaking residents in Ecuador, for after all it is one of those tropical countries, where the easiest life, or at least existence, is to be had, where the soil is enormously fertile and the climate delightful. In the present age a laborious life is detested, and thousands have left their homes in the Eastern States and Canada for the attractions of this nature which California possesses. Why such people should not go further and fare even better as regards soil, climate, and natural productions, is not very apparent. The truth probably is that the further one goes southward from the latitude of 45°; and the more the natural advantages increase, the greater is the moral deterioration of the natives, and the more rapid would probably be the degeneration of the immigrants. The advantages of such a country resemble somewhat the natural powers of mind in the possession of a man of talent; application and perseverance are necessary to develope them, and that is usually possessed by the inhabitants of northern countries, and by the man of mediocre ability, in greater degree than by the indolent southerner, or the heaven-born genius.

V.—HOMEWARD BOUND.

"Happy are the people that are in such a case : yea, blessed are the people who have the Lord for their God." Psalm cxliv. 15.

On the 1st June I bade good-bye to Guayaquil. Although my intercourse with the natives of Ecuador had been pleasant enough, still I never could rid myself of a feeling of insecurity when on shore, and therefore felt heartily glad when I found myself on board the "Islay," in the Guayaquil river, and bound for Panama. As I remarked to the captain, "the next best thing to being on British soil is to "be on board a British ship." The "Islay" also belongs to the South Pacific Steam Navigation Company, and a Scotsman would suppose that it is named after one of the western islands of his native country. This is not so however; the name is pronounced as spelt, aud belongs to an inland locality of Peru. The "Islay" weighed anchor before breakfast time, steamed up the west side of the river to a point opposite the western limit of the town, then with her helm hard to starboard, swept beautifully round in the broad stream, and was soon speeding rapidly down with the tide to the Pacific. She had however to stop in her course and put ashore an unlucky native who had come on board accompanying a passenger. This is quite a regular occurrence when these steamers are leaving port. Natives *will* come on board, and, although warned by bells and whistles, will not leave till the very last minute. In this respect they very much resemble French Canadians, who behave exactly in the same manner on board railway cars.

The Latin races seem to like the stir and fuss of this sort of thing even although it brings them little profit and some loss, for it frequently happens, both with Spaniards and Frenchmen, that they are carried off by steamer or car a stage further than they bargained for.

The "Islay," after reaching the Pacific, made straight for Panama, and during almost the whole of the passage kept out of sight of land. The weather was dull, the sea troubled with a ground swell, and heavy showers were not unfrequent. It was certainly not so pleasant as when we sailed southward, but officers and passengers were very agreeable. Among the latter were many Spaniards, and plenty of Germans, besides a Californian mining man and a Yankee colonel, both returning from Peru. The Californian was a round-faced, bullet-headed, good natured sort of a man, but he swore more terribly even than " our troops in Flanders." He used most frequently and in the most unnecessary manner the names most sacred to a Christian, and at last I asked him whether he would consider himself justified if he were groping about in the dark in giving the first person he met a slap in the face. He looked surprised as he slowly said, " No. What do you mean?" I answered : " When you swear in that way you " are unconsciously dealing blows around you which strike "and hurt many people in their most sacred beliefs."

"Well, I think you exaggerate," said he, "but I am afraid "you are right. No one should use expressions which have " no meaning."

" There is meaning enough in the terms you use."

" There is none to me, and I really must give up swearing "by what I don't believe in."

" Then you mean to say you don't believe in the Almighty, "the Saviour, heaven or hell?"

"Exactly so. Nor in a hereafter, nor in anything I cannot understand."

"There is one thing you cannot understand, but must believe in."

"What is that?"

"Death."

"That is a fact, and easily understood."

"Let us see. What dies? The body or the spirit?"

"Both."

"Then you maintain that the spirit is at once blotted out of existence?"

"Of course."

"And the constituents of the body also?"

"I cannot say that."

"I thought not; they merely change their form?"

"Yes."

"And why should a different fate await the spirit?"

"Well, I have not studied that question."

"Then you cannot maintain that you understand the nature of death, which you must believe in?"

"Well, I know at any rate this: that I was brought into this world without being consulted, and when I am taken away I shall probably be taken care of, but I don't think my spirit will trouble any body, and I am not bound to look after it."

"You are certainly the person most interested, and its existence is a matter of greater importance to you than any worldly business can be."

"But it is so difficult to figure about it."

"Look here! There was surely a time when it had no existence?"

"Yes."

"Was not its being brought into being an act of creation?"

"I suppose so."

"And does not science teach us that matter once set in motion cannot be arrested; that anything once created cannot be annihilated?"

"I believe so."

"And why should not that apply to your living spirit as well as to dead matter?"

"Why, you bore it into a fellow dreadfully."

After that Mr. Bullethead rather avoided me, and probably put me down as a parson, but I think his figures of speech became somewhat less florid. When, subsequently, the conversation turned on mining affairs, I found that he had formerly been the superintendent of an extensive mine in Nevada, and more recently had been engaged in the manufacture of ice in Lima. He indulged in strong expressions of contempt for the "Indian Governments" of South America, and in sweeping condemnation of ecclesiastical abuses. According to him the conduct of the Roman Catholic clergy was in some cases utterly shameful and shameless, while the state of society generally he characterised as exceedingly corrupt. This last point was disputed by the Colonel, who maintained that many people who criticised Peruvian society adversely were exactly those whose opportunities of observation were limited, and who had never obtained the entrée into the best families. He admitted that the priests were no better than they should be, and that it was principally the female sex who were under religious influence, but denied that any general imputation could be justly made against their virtue and fair fame.

The political affairs of Peru were also brought up, and the Colonel was very severe on the speculators, as he called them, who had inveigled the government into its disastrous railway policy. Mr. Bullethead took the opposite view, blaming Peruvians, high in station, whom those same speculators had to bribe before they could obtain contracts. Even the Archbishop of Lima, he maintained, had a finger in the pie. But it appears, too, that the entire Peruvian official world, civil service, army and navy, are far too numerous; that the average Peruvian disdains work and assumes that his government is bound to provide for him, and that this is another source of financial derangement. I enquired what the army and navy were about.

"The army is always ready to make or mar pronuncia-"mentos and revolutions," answered Mr. Bullethead.

"The navy lies idle in the harbour of Callao," said the Colonel.

"Yes; I remember to have seen the armed ships there "with their lounging idle crews," I remarked, "and I think " that you Americans ought to be glad that 'Britannia still "'rules the waves.'"

"How so?"

"What else prevents those same ships in Callao harbour "from becoming pirates?"

"Nothing, after all, except the police of the high seas," admitted the Colonel.

"What a pity there are not international constables on "land as well," said Mr. Bullethead.

The conversation at the dinner table of the "Islay" on the 2nd inst. became very lively while a recent case of manslaughter at Tumaco, in New Granada, was being discussed. A native had been killed by an English trader in self-defence, and the latter had been sent to Bogota, the capital, partly to insure his safety from the populace, and partly that his case might be justly disposed of. In the conversation, the native character was pretty well discussed and condemned as a compound of vice, cowardice, and treachery. I then remarked to the captain: "This coast "seems as much in need of missionaries as Africa or "Melanesia."

"They have priest enough," said the Captain, "if that "would do them any good."

"Yes," said a German opposite, "missionaries are only "good for making people believe musty doctrines, and the "priests can do that well enough."

"Missionaries can do better than that," said I, "they "have often enough shewn savages the example of a brave "and unselfish life."

"But you must enlighten them," maintained Mr. Krause, "and show them the benefits of civilisation before talking "to them about religion."

"I fear," said I, "that your plan would produce a mon-"ster, whom you would be unable to control afterwards."

"You seem to think," said Bullethead, "that no country "can get along without ministers, or Sunday school, or "something of that sort."

"I certainly think that without some such agencies a "country cannot last long. The essential parts of a "nation are family, church, and state; and if any of these "are faulty the result will be a lame community."

Here I had mounted my hobby, and every one seemed anxious to get out of its way except Mr. Krause, the German, who accompanied me on deck, and expressed his surprise at hearing such sentiments in the present enlightened age. He further enquired whether I had read Strauss' latest work, "The New and the Old Faith,"* evidently expecting that liberal-minded thinkers would receive it as unquestioningly as Christians do the Holy

---

* Der neue und der alte Glaube: Bonn; 1873.

Scriptures. Mr. Krause seemed surprised when I told him that I was well acquainted with the "Confession" of the arch sceptic, and he did not seem to be aware that it had elicited from some of his countrymen the most able and convincing replies. I asserted that the last paragraph of Strauss' work contained in itself almost a refutation of the views put forward by the author, and our dispute on this point was long and warm, and culminated in a discussion as to the practical effect of Strauss' teaching.

"After all," said I, "what would be the gain of believing in Strauss' *Universum* instead of God?"

"Gain!" exclaimed Mr. Krause.

"Yes, gain," said I. "Suppose a modern nation were, like Strauss and his disciples, to repudiate the name Christian—to cry, 'Great is *das Universum*, and Strauss is his (or its?) prophet!'—and, in place of Church and Bible, to substitute history, poetry, and music, Where would be the advantage or improvement?"

"The greatest advantage would be in the acknowledgement of the truth."

"But the point in dispute is, What is the truth? and practical people are inclined to judge of the correctness of a principle by the fruits which it produces. Would, for instance, your 'new faith' make men more brave or women more virtuous?"

"I believe it would."

"Then state an instance from history as a proof."

"The 'new faith' is not old enough for that."

"And yet," said I, "without being able to prove your case from past experience, you ask us to aid you in obliterating the religious sentiment of a nation, an agency for good the most powerful the world has ever seen."

"For evil as much as good, I imagine," said Mr. Krause.

"No, not so much," I maintained. " Look at the deeds of the Romans so long as they believed in their old heathen deities. Look at what the Arabs became under the influence of Mohammedanism. Then, in your own country, during the Thirty Years war, what enabled the Swedish infantry to resist the charge of Pappenheim's dragoons, seven times repeated, at the battle of Leipsic?"

"The remembrance of the sack of Madgeburg, perhaps."

"Not so much, for they were not Germans. Their stout hearts were still more strengthened by gathering round their chaplains for morning and evening prayer."

"Brave men are not always religious."

"Perhaps not; but true religion converts cowards into brave men. Even your countrymen, during the last war, are, in the '*Wacht am Rhein*,' said to be 'upright. pious and strong,'* which is a description of a thoroughly religious character. *There* was the strength of the Fatherland, and the want of that same character was the weakness of France."

But Mr. Krause held tenaciously to his ideas, and I found it useless to try to enlighten the enlightened in their own conceit. But, nevertheless, there is little danger of the North Germans accepting the new gospel according to Strauss, and, in that respect, little to fear for their future as a nation.

We reached Panama on the 4th June and obtained the same quarters that we formerly had in the Grand Central Hotel, from which we had a full view of the Plaza and the cathedral, and could observe how indefatigable priests and people were in their religious observances. In our strolls towards the outskirts we could also observe that Panama,

---

* "Der Deutsche bieder, fromm und stark
"Beschutzt die heil'ge Landesmark."

like Guayaquil, was sadly in need of sewers and scavengers, although the black condors were very plentiful and active. Panama is also deformed by the number of its ruins. Every street has its roofless houses, and not unfrequently these are old churches or monastic establishments. The expulsion of the Jesuits cannot have been an unmixed good to the community if it produced such fruits as these roofless, deserted buildings. They are mostly of sandstone, which is very much weather-worn, but the mortar must have been of excellent quality, for it stands out like quartz veins at the joints.

On the 6th I started from Panama to cross the Isthmus, and before leaving I parted from Armstrong, who proposed to return to San Francisco. He was not very demonstrative, but fervently expressed the hope that we might meet again in South America, his favorite spot being the Valley of the Cauca, in New Granada, which, he thinks, will yet eclipse all the other tropical states in agricultural and mineral productions.

The railway ride across the Isthmus is a very interesting but very expensive one, $20 being charged for a distance of forty miles. Natives are carried at much lower rates, and this is probably the only railway in the world where the fares discriminate against foreigners. The company owning the railway no doubt obtain their share of the profit, but most of it goes as revenue to the Government of New Granada. The usual luxuriant tropical vegetation, and some picturesque mountains are to be seen in crossing the Isthmus, but these were tame to me after having penetrated the Guayaquil lowland and scaled the Andes. The most of the local passengers, as we near Aspinwall, are the negroes of the country, here, singularly enough, called "Jamaica niggers." Whether this indicates a peculiar species or merely origin it is hard to say. So much is certain, however, that they are very loudly dressed, very loud-mannered, and more insolent and independent negroes are not to be found elsewhere.

In the evening we reached Aspinwall, or as it is now called by the authorities, "Colon," in honor of the discoverer of the new world. The most notable object in the place is a superb bronze statue of Christopher Columbus, apparently in the act of protecting an Indian. It is at the same time a standard whereby to measure the degree of admiration entertained by the Government and natives for the fine arts. It is only raised about a foot above the ground, and the pedestal of *red brick* is in a very bad state of repair. At the point where the railway passengers alight in Colon, for there does not appear to be any station, a row of brick buildings runs parallel with the railway track, and, in the evening, this street presents a lively scene; one singular feature in it being the number of gambling tables, covered with green cloth, placed in the open air, at which passers by are invited to try their luck. Gambling seems to be regarded as a matter of course and a legitimate occupation in these latitudes, for in Panama, at the Grand Hotel, there is a *rouge et noir* table close to the bar-room. At Colon, negroes, sailors and foreigners, patronise the institution, and it is related that a native of Central America once strayed northward as far as San Francisco, and very much missed in that city his favorite, publicly exposed, and green covered tables. At last he was overjoyed to stumble over one, or at least a box covered with green cloth, from which the proprietor ground out very inviting music. This the stranger thought was the means adopted in northern latitudes for attracting customers, and piece after piece of his money he placed on the green music table, which was quietly swept off by the proprietor. It was some time before the would-be gambler was made to understand that he had been giving, not gambling, his money away.

Shortly after reaching Colon I went on board the steamer "Andes," bound for New York. Her cargo seemed to consist almost entirely of bananas, and the loading of these by a noisy and half naked crowd of negroes went on till far into the night, much interfering with my repose in a stateroom below. I therefore slept until late next morning, and then found, by the motion of the ship, that she was out on the Caribbean sea, and that I was experiencing the roughest weather I had yet encountered since I left home. I felt still more uncomfortable on recollecting that this sea of cannibals, as the early discoverers in their unfounded terror named it, might turn out a cannibal sea in so far as concerned our good ship and the carcases of her passengers. The gale was quite severe from the southeast, and not a passenger appeared on deck for the first two days. Then the storm subsided, and after passing Jamaica, the steamer called at the island of Navasa, lying off the west end of San Domingo, on the 9th June. This island is said to be solely occupied by a colony of Americans, entirely of the male sex, and of latent filibustering principles. Navasa is supposed to belong to the Republic of Hayti, but this claim, it is said, the colonists are prepared to resist.

Next day, in going through the Windward Passage, and in sailing past the east end of Cuba, we enjoyed delightful weather. All the passengers appeared at meals and on deck, and after reconnoitering engaged each other in mutual civilities and conversation. My old acquaintance, Mr. Bullethead, was among them, and some familiar faces turned up belonging to Spanish passengers, who had also come north by the "Islay." Then there were strange faces from the neighbourhood of Panama—a Dr. Williamson, resident in a town on the Isthmus, but of English parentage; a couple of South American medical students, bound for Göttingen; and an Irishman named Kelly, on his way back from the state of Antiochia, in New Granada, where he had been "prospecting" for gold, in the interest of certain New York gentlemen.

As a matter of course, Kelly, Bullethead, and I were quickly drawn together by our common interest in mining affairs. Kelly's experience in New Granada, while hunting up gold claims and locating them under the Spanish mining law, and his description of his intercourse among the officials and with the natives, was listened to with interest. He was very successful in obtaining the confidence both of Indians and Spaniards, and their priests, for he was himself a Roman Catholic. Learning this, I asked him whether all that I had heard as regards the immorality prevailing among the clergy was true. He reluctantly admitted that it was, adding, "They are not priests." Dr. Williamson, who also turned out to be a Roman Catholic, confirmed Kelly's evidence; but maintained that an improvement was taking place, owing to the efforts of the new Bishop of Panama. Strange to say, this condition of things did not seem to influence their opinions very much, for they were as loyal and enthusiastic in defence of their church as if no abuses whatever existed in it.

I put it to the doctor whether there was not something extremely inconsistent, or at any rate ill-timed, in the recent assumption of infallibility on the part of the head of the church while such a large section of it was in such a terrible state of demoralisation. But his faith was too colossal to be, in the slightest degree, shaken by the reflection. Indeed, I speedily found in him an uncompromising defender of ultramontanism and the present extreme pretensions of the Papacy. Of course he came into immediate conflict with Mr. Bullethead, who insisted that the South American republics were being overdosed with religion.

"I don't suppose your government is much troubled with religion," said the doctor.

"We don't want any," said Bullethead.

"Don't you? and on what does the authority of your government rest?"

"On the will of the people," was the ready reply.

"And so it is the will of the people that confers upon your executive the power to declare war and punish criminals by hanging?" asked the doctor.

"Certainly," said Bullethead.

"But how can a society of individuals convey that which none of them possess? How can a man bestow upon his ruler the power of taking away life, when he himself has no such right?"

"Each individual may not have the power; but as an aggregate, and as a fact, they have. Look at what the Vigilantes did in San Francisco."

"Still these were extraordinary proceedings, which they themselves acknowledged to be illegal," argued the doctor.

"Then I cannot see whence any government derives its powers," said Bullethead.

"Because light has been denied you," said the doctor; "but it is very simple to us, 'The powers that be are ordained of God.'"

"Including, I suppose, the United States government," remarked Bullethead.

"That is very doubtful, seeing that it almost expressly disclaims any such authorisation."

"You would not then," I asked, "deny a legal status to any government which acknowledges God as the ruler of all nations, and the source of all its powers?"

"It would be necessary for them also to show some visible title, and that can only be obtained from the head of the church, the representative of God upon earth."

"I thought it would come to that. 'L'Eglise c'est moi,' is the language of the Pope," said I; "then governments which are not sanctioned by Rome have no legal existence?"

"That is my understanding of the matter," said the doctor, uncompromisingly.

"And the church being the source of civil power is superior to the state?"

"No doubt."

"I am quite willing to admit the correctness of part of your theory; that all power is from on high, and as scripture teaches us, that Jesus Christ is 'King of kings and Lord of 'lords.' But is not, in the bible, and even in your theology, the church represented as the Bride of the Messiah?"

"Yes, the pure and invisible church is so regarded."

"Would it not therefore be logical to regard the visible church as standing in the same relation to the visible state?"

"How do you mean?"

"The state, deriving its authority from Christ the ruler of nations, ought to acknowledge and protect the visible church as its spouse."

"Well?"

"Then of course the church is subject to the state as a wife is to her husband."

"You have exactly reversed the proper relation," said the doctor

"Only in accordance with your own theory," said I. "You, however, wish to see the state henpecked by the church, while I wish it to be honored and protected by the state, as a gentle and virtuous wife is by a good and brave husband."

" That has a very pretty sound," said Kelly, " and almost captivates me, for then, you see, the church as the wife and mother would take charge of the children."

" That would no doubt logically follow," said I, "but she would have to rear them up to be loyal and obedient subjects to her husband the state, even although he should happen to be a protestant.

" Or else she would have to suffer bodily coercion by a Bismarck," added the doctor.

" Well; that would at any rate place education on a religious foundation," said Kelly, "and that is what catholics have been always striving for."

"Yes," said the doctor, " we have always maintained that mind and spirit should each have a degree of attention paid to their development, proportionate to their relative importance. Therefore man's spiritual nature should have most time devoted to its cultivation. After that comes mental training."

" I fear your practice does not always sustain your theory. Where are the spiritual wants of your people attended to?"

"In the church and confessional, and in our convents."

" Those are more generally for the women, and intended to guide and control their affections and emotions," I argued, "but how about the males. Where are your schools, colleges and universities?"

"They are not required for spiritual, but for intellectual culture," maintained the doctor.

" But surely the mind and judgment must be placed higher
" than the heart of man, since its imagination is evil from
" his youth ?"

" They cannot be placed higher than his spirit or soul."

" O, do let us avoid metaphysics ; are not your clergy in
" many countries trained in colleges and universities?"

" Yes," the doctor admitted.

" And are not the universities sometimes established by
" the state?"

" Admitted !"

" And is not the culture of the mind and intellect of man
" the chief object of these higher institutions; and are not
" your clergy, after having their intellects so trained, placed
" in positions to guide others, and especially those whose
" natures are impulsive and emotional?"

" And what then ?"

" Does not this then prove that man's mind or reason is
" intended to rule his merely emotional nature, or his heart?"

" That is rather far-fetched."

" Perhaps ; but it is quite consistent. The state is the
" minister of God, and can prove its title to be so regarded,
" much better than the Pope can prove that he is the Vicar
" of Christ. The state establishes, supports and protects
" the church, and commissions it to effect among the people
" that change of heart or conversion of the soul which is
" the true object of all religious teaching."

" I see you are bound to place the state uppermost," said the doctor, evidently tired of the discussion, the latter part of which we had all to ourselves. Kelly and Bullethead had long since had recourse to cards, and were absorbed and excited in the mysteries and chances of euchre.

On the 11th June, after getting through the Crooked island passage, we came in sight of Watlings Island, or

San Salvador, where Columbus first landed in 1492. In spite of its historical interest, it did not seem to be regarded by any of the passengers with extraordinary curiosity, but I could not refrain from asking the doctor how much of the immense territory then conveyed by the Pope to Spain now remained in its possession. The doctor retorted that the greater part of it was still Spanish in language and Catholic in religion, and that quite possibly Spanish Americans might yet astonish the world. Senores Galves and Cornejo, the medical students, were not, however, very enthusiastic in speaking of their native country and its prospects, and much preferred, in conversation with me, to talk of Göttingen and its professors. They were able to give me many interesting particulars regarding Wöhler and Von Waltershausen, both of them now in the " sear and yellow leaf." I found they were much more fluent in German than I was in Spanish, and we always ended our talks in the former language. They had evidently passed through some of the phases of German "*Burschenleben*," and both their faces bore proof of their having stood upon the "*Mensur*," or duelling ground. I made mention of this to the doctor. " Your friends have " been duelling as well as studying in Germany."

" No ! why do you think so ?"

" Why, look at the scars on their faces."

" You are surely mistaken," said the doctor; but he found on enquiry, subsequently, that it was even so, and then expressed his surprise at the circumstance, adding that he could not see why people should flock to Germany for education.

" If the English are a nation of shop-keepers, the Germans " are a nation of pedagogues," said I, but the doctor listened very incredulously to me as I recounted the advantages of studying and even living in Germany. He was plainly prejudiced against the Fatherland, and at last remarked: "I suppose, too, that that is the country where your ideal state is to be found that protects its spouse, the Church, so carefully and governs it so wisely."

"No," said I, "there you are mistaken. Prussia is not quite my model nation in that respect, for there two churches exist, whose relations with the state more resemble bigamy than honest marriage."

The doctor became interested, and I went on to explain to him how Protestant union was accomplished in Germany nearly sixty years ago. On the third centenary of the Reformation, Frederick William III. of Prussia invited the Lutheran and Reformed Churches to unite. The idea was joyously adopted, and the followers of Luther and Calvin combined in the most of the German States to form a "Protestant Evangelical Church." This would be equivalent to a union of Episcopalians and Presbyterians here, of which there is very little immediate prospect. This union in Prussia had the result of placing Protestantism side by side with Roman Catholicism as a state religion, or of establishing a double State Church, with a double set of ecclesiastical officials, churches and schools. In the latter there were the regular hours for "religion" just as for arithmetic, and the state undertook to train the children of Roman Catholic parents, and those of the Protestant persuasion, in their respective religions. This system of "concurrent endowment" did not, however, always run smoothly, but that was chiefly owing to the unreasonable interference of the Pope in the matter of "mixed marriages." In fact, the King of Prussia, although he enriched the Roman Catholic clergy, and built them churches and schools, received as little thanks then as Mr. Gladstone has in our own day.

"Well, I was sorry," said the doctor, "that Gladstone's

" University Bill did not become law, but his subsequent
" action has shewn that he merits no thanks from the
" Catholic Church."

" From the Pope, you mean."

" No, from the Church, for he has done his best to shew
" that the Catholic Church, like other religious bodies,
" changes its doctrines to suit the times."

" Well, I think he succeeded in proving that very plainly.
" The Church or Pope decreed the doctrine of Papal
" Infallibility, which was not previously an article of the
" Catholic faith."

" You're mistaken there," interposed Kelly, "that doctrine
" was always held by true Catholics, although it was not
" publicly promulgated."

" Then, why did the Bishops of the Irish Church declare
" in 1810 that the infallibility of the Pope was not a part
" of the Catholic religion?"

Kelly looked at the doctor, who tacitly admitted the fact, but maintained that the declaration of certain Irish Bishops could not bind the Church.

" They certainly were unable to influence the council,
" although they tried," said I.

" Did they though?" asked Kelley.

"Of course; but they were put down by the Italian
"bishops. There's oppression for you! Why don't you
" agitate for ' Home rule ' in the church as well as in state?
" Why don't the Fenians march against Rome ?"

" Oh! now you are joking," said Kelly. "Faith! the
" Fenians have their hands full just now. Never before
" were there in New York such a large number of unem·
" ployed workmen, and many an Irishman I know who has
" all he can do to keep his children from starving."

" Why don't you shoot the landlords," I asked.

"There! you're joking again; but we mean to turn out "the Republicans and that will help us."

"Why; the Republicans are protectionists, and have been "providing you all the time with work."

"And what does their protection amount to?" asked Kelly, who was a ship-carpenter by trade. "It has ruined "shipbuilding and all the machine and marine works of "New York."

The conversation continued, but the philosophical dialogue on the theory of government and church connection degenerated into a discussion on party politics in the United States.

We experienced very fine weather on the Atlantic, and conversation certainly did not flag. And besides, Bullethead and I had each discovered in the other a "foeman worthy of our steel" at chess, and this supplied us with abundant recreation all the way to New York. I found, however, that my opponent was inclined to be very liberal as regards the rules of chess, insisting upon their relaxation in many particulars. In consequence of this, unsatisfactory playing and even disputes resulted. Hereupon, I endeavoured to shew him the beauty of conservatism and the danger of tampering with existing law and practice, not only in chess, but in politics. I further twitted him with being like his government, impatient of international law, when it seemed to interfere even temporarily with his interests. But Mr. Bullethead had become less belligerent, and was not to be provoked, not even when the doctor said:

"The people of the United States pride themselves on "having cut away their government from all the experience "of other nations, and now it is adrift on the ocean "without compass, and even shuts its eyes to the truths "told by the everlasting stars."

"It has only eyes for the stars and stripes," I remarked.

"*My* stars! what do you mean?" exclaimed Bullethead.

"Your government has no church to keep and guide its conscience," answered the doctor.

"No," continued I, "in the United States husband and wife, church and state, are divorced and live in separate establishments."

"Oh, I see!" said Bullethead, "you are still on the hunt after your model state with its submissive church."

"That's so!" said the doctor, "where *is* this model community of yours after all, where the union of church and state is so perfect?"

"The nearest approach to perfection in this matter," I answered, "is to be found in England."

"What! where the most crying injustice is perpetrated against Catholics and Dissenters."

"Still," I remarked, "there the church occupies my favorite position, acknowledging the state as its head, and it seems to me that if ever a union of Christians throughout the realm is to take place, it will be upon the broad platform of the Church of England."

"To me, on the contrary," maintained the doctor, "it appears that the current of opinion is rather towards complete disestablishment."

"So it would seem," said I, "but I believe that there is still statesmanship enough left in England to prevent such a lame and impotent conclusion."

"People are getting very extravagant now-a-days," said the doctor, "there is not much repairing done; if anything gets leaky or damaged they throw it away and begin with a bran new article."

"That may apply to France and South America, but not to thrifty and practical England."

"But what would you do with the Dissenters, Presbyterians and Catholics?"

"Exempt them and their property from taxation for the support of the Episcopal Church," I replied. "Confer upon them the power to tax themselves for the support of their own."

"And the Episcopalians you would put exactly in the same position?"

"Pretty much."

"Then you would establish the sects, and the Church of England would be practically dis-established."

"Not at all; but I would establish the Christian Church, allow each branch to support itself, and give to each a legal standing. I would also so legislate that each would be obliged to take charge of the education of its own people, and the support of its own poor; subject, of course, to supervision on the part of the state."

"And that you would call honourable matimony?" asked the doctor.

"Certainly; of the whole British Empire with the whole Christian Church."

"To me it looks remarkably like polygamy."

"These various churches and sects are one in doctrine and discipline, and if it is possible for Lessing to maintain that the Jewish, Mahometan and Christian religions are indistinguishable in spirit, I may surely be permitted to do the same as regards the branches of the Christian Church."

Here I was obliged to give the doctor, Kelly and Bullethead a *viva voce* translation from memory of Lessing's well-known analogy. I deem it profitable here to introduce it, in the form of a translation of the 5th Scene of the second Act of "Nathan the Wise," a dramatic poem written by Gotthold Ephraim Lessing in 1779. It may be named :

THE SULTAN AND THE SAGE.

SALADIN (seated) :
Tread hither, Jew ! come nigher ! come quite nigh,
Come without fear !

NATHAN :
That leave I to thy foes,

SALADIN :
Thy name is Nathan ?

NATHAN :
Yes.

SALADIN :
Nathan the Wise?

NATHAN :
No, no.

SALADIN :
Well, then, the people name thee so.

NATHAN :
'Tis possible, the people !

SALADIN :
Thou dost not
Believe that I would treat contemptuously
The people's voice ? Long have I wished to know
The man whom it called wise.

NATHAN :
But if it were
Merely in scorn the people named me thus ?
If to the people wisdom were no more
Than prudence ? And the prudent man no more
Than one who was alive to his own gain ?

SALADIN :
To his true gain, thou meanest ?

NATHAN :
Then indeed
The most unselfish were the prudentest,
Prudence and wisdom quite equality.

SALADIN :
I hear thee prove what thou wouldst fain gainsay.
The people know man's true advantage not,
But thou dost know ; at least to know hast sought ;
Hast well considered ; that alone makes wise.

NATHAN :
Which each one thinks he is.

SALADIN:
                    Well! well! enough
Of modesty! To hear it constantly
Where one expects dry reason but disgusts. (He rises.)
Let us to business; to the point! But, Jew,
Thou must be upright!—upright and sincere!

NATHAN:
Sultan! I'll surely serve thee so that I
Of further favors may be worthy found.

SALADIN:
Serve me? and how?

NATHAN:
                    Thou mayst select the best
Of all I have and at the lowest price.

SALADIN:
What dost thou mean? Thou speakest of thy wares,
But with the trader I have nought to do.

NATHAN:
Then thou perhaps wouldst know if I perceived
Ought on my way of movements of the foe,
Who certainly again bestirs himself.

SALADIN:
Nor yet of that wish I thy speech; of that
I know as much already as does suit
My purposes. In short;—

NATHAN:
                    Command me, Sultan.

SALADIN:
I seek thy teaching in another thing,
In quite another matter;—since thou art
So wise; then tell me once for all what faith
Or what religion seems to thee the best?

NATHAN:
I am a Jew.

SALADIN:
                    And I a Mussulman.
The Christian stands between us. Of these three
Religions one alone is real and true.
A man like thee remains not where the chance
Of birth has cast his lot; or if he does,
It is because of grounds, born of deep thought
And ripe consideration; of wise choice.
Well, then! Impart thy wise experience.
Let me perceive the reasons which to seek
I've lack'd the time, and let me understand
The choice determined by these reasons, so
That I may make it mine. Thou startest! How?

Thou weigh'st me with thine eye? Perchance I am
The first of Sultans who has such a whim,
Which, nevertheless seems not to me beneath
A Sultan's thoughts. Is it not so? Then speak!
Or wishest thou a moment's time to thiuk?
I'll give it thee. Consider well and with
All speed. I quickly shall return. [*Exit.*]

     NATHAN (*alone*).
        'Tis strange!
'Tis wonderful! What does the Sultan wish?
With money I come well prepared, and
He doth wish for truth! so solid and so bright,—
As if the truth were coin! Ah! if 'twere but
Ancient coin which custom was to weigh! Yes!
That still were possible! But such new coin
Which but th' impression makes; which on the board
May just be counted out! That is not truth!
As money from the counter to the bag,
So would he sweep pure truth into the brain!
Who is just now the Jew, then? He or I?
But how, if he should not demand the truth
In truth? 'Tis true indeed that to suspect
Him of his using truth as but a trap
Were far too low!—too low! What is it, then,
That is too low for an exalted one?
'Tis sure! 'tis certain! he did rudely plunge
Into the house. A friend knocks, listens first.
I must walk carefully. But how? but how?
To be a stubborn Jew will not avail,
And not at all a Jew, still less. Because
If not a Jew, he only has to ask
Why not a Mussulman? I have it now!
That sure will save me! Others than children
Have been fed with tales! He comes! I'm ready!

[*Enter Saladin.*]   SALADIN:
Am I too quick returned? Thou'rt at an end
With thy consideration? Well, then, speak!
There's not a soul to hear us.

     NATHAN:
      Why should not
The whole world hear us?

     SALADIN:
      Ah! Is Nathan, then,
So certain of his case? That I call wise!
Ne'er to conceal the truth! To hazard all
Upon it! Life and body! House and goods!

NATHAN:
Yes! when 'tis of use and necessary.

SALADIN:
From now, then, I may hope to bear the name,
Improver of the world and of the law,
With justice.

NATHAN:
'Tis a name most beautiful.
Yet, Sultan, ere I quite confide in thee
Permit that I relate a story first.

SALADIN:
Why not? I've always been a friend of tales
Well told.

NATHAN:
Yes! but to tell them well, I fear,
Is scarce a trade of mine.

SALADIN:
Again thou art
So proudly modest? Quick! go on! relate!

NATHAN:
Grey years ago a man liv'd in the East,
Who did possess a ring of worth immense
From a beloved hand. Opal the stone
Which play'd a hundred bright and beauteous hues
And had the secret power to make belov'd
And pleasing both to God and man, the man
Who wore it in this faith and confidence.
No wonder, then, that this man in the East
Would ne'er allow the ring to leave his hand,
And did arrange forever to retain
It in his family, and in this way:
He left the ring unto his best lov'd son;
And did ordain that he should it bequeath
Unto his dearest son, and that thenceforth
This dearest son, without respect of birth,
Should be, in virtue of the ring alone,
The head, the prince of all his family.
Thou understandest, Sultan?

SALADIN:
Yes. Go on!

NATHAN:
The ring transmitted thus from son to son
Came to a father of three sons at last
Who all to him alike obedient were,
And all of whom he therefore equally
Could not but love. From time to time, indeed,

The one ; sometimes the other ; then the third,
(As each did sep'rately converse with him
And the two other brothers could not share
His outpoured heart) did each successively
Appear to him more worthy of the ring,
Which also he the pious weakness had
To promise each of them successively.
But finally the father's time of death
Arrives and with it great perplexity.
It pains him so to hurt two of his sons
Who on his word depend.   What, then, to do ?
He sends in secret to a jeweller
And gives instructions for two other rings
According to the pattern of his own,
And bids him spare no cost or workmanship
To make them perfectly resemble it.
In this the artist quite succeeds, and when
He brings the rings the father can himself
No more distinguish the original.
Content and happy now, he calls his sons,
And gives them each, in secret, one by one,
His benediction, and a ring,—and dies.
Sultan ! thou hearest still ?

SALADIN :
     I hear! I hear !
Come with thy tale now quickly to an end.

NATHAN :
'Tis ended, for what follows may be well
Divin'd.   Scarce was the father dead, when each
Comes with his ring, and each demands to be
The ruler of the house.   They then enquire,
Complain, dispute.   In vain ; the genuine ring
Could not be proved.

[*After a pause, in which he awaits the Sultan's answer*] :
    As little proved, as now
The true religion can be proved to us.

SALADIN :
And that's the answer to my enquiry ?

NATHAN :
'Tis merely my excuse if I believe
Myself incompetent to tell the rings
The which the father purposely contrived
That they should never be distinguished.

SALADIN :
The rings ! Jest not with me ! I should have thought
That the religions which I named to thee

Were quick distinguished; even to the clothes,—
Aye, to their meat and drink.

NATHAN:
                    But surely not,
If only we recall their origin.
Are they not founded all on history,
Traditional or written, and all such
Must surely be received in faith? Well, then,
Whose faith or truth does one love least to doubt?
Surely the truth of those whose blood runs in
Our veins! Who, from our childhood up,
Have given us proof of love and tenderness?
Who ne'er deceived us otherwise than when
'Twas better far for us to be deceived?
How can I less believe mine ancestors
Than thou dost thine? Or in the other case,
Can I demand from thee that thou shouldst give
The lie unto thy fathers, and their faith,
In order not to contradict mine own?
The same applieth to the Christian. Not?

SULTAN:
(By the All Living One! The man says true.
I must be dumb.)

NATHAN:
                    Let's to the rings return;
The sons accused each other; came before
The Judge, to whom each swore that he received
His ring direct from out his father's hand;
Which was quite true! That he had long possessed
His father's promise that he should enjoy
The rights and privileges of the ring,—
Also quite true! The father, each affirm'd
Could not have been deceitful towards him,
And rather than allow a thing so foul
To be suspected of his father dear,
He would, although always inclined to think
The best of his dear brethren, be obliged
To think them guilty of the falsest play,
And that he soon would know how to unmask
The traitors, and besides revenge himself.

SALADIN:
And now, the Judge! I do demand to know
What thou dost make the Judge pronounce. Speak on!

NATHAN:
The Judge spoke thus: If ye do not present
The father quick before this tribunal

I shall discharge you all. Do ye then think
That I sit here to guess at enigmas?
Or do ye wait until the real ring
Does ope its mouth? But stop! Ye all have said
That this same ring contains the magic power
To make its owner lov'd by God and man.
That must decide! The false rings cannot have
This virtue. Now, who is the most belov'd
Of his two brethren? Tell me quick! Ye're dumb?
The rings work only inward! not without!
Each one most fondly loves himself the most?
Then are ye all deceivers and deceived!
Your rings, all three, are false, and the true ring
Most likely has been lost. The father, then,
In order to repair and hide the loss
For one ring substituted three.

SALADIN:
Glorious!

NATHAN:
And so, the Judge continued, if ye wish
Not my advice but my decision,—go!
But my advice is this: Take now this thing
Exactly as it lies. If each of you
In truth a ring received from your sire,
Let each believe his ring th' authentic one.
Perhaps the father would not tolerate
The one ring's tyranny within his house!
And certain 'tis that he did love you all,
And equally, and wish'd to punish none.
Let each conceive and foster zealously
A love unbribed and free from prejudice!
Let each of you as for a wager strive
To shew the power before the light of day
Which rests within the stone of his own ring.
Assist this power with gentleness and truth,
With meekness, candour and benevolence;
With most sincere devotion unto God,
And when the virtues of the ring at last
Do clearly manifest themselves among
Your children's children and their progeny:
After a thousand thousand years have past
I do invite you here before this seat.
When that time comes a wiser one than I
Shall here preside and judge. Now, go in peace!
So said the modest Judge. If, Sultan, thou
Dost feel thyself to be this promised one,
This wiser one—

SALADIN:
    I? Dust and ashes! No!
NATHAN:
What ails thee, Sultan?
SALADIN:
    Nathan! Nathan, dear!
The thousand thousand years thy Judge pronounced
Are not yet past; nor is his judgment seat
For Saladin.

In this poem, Lessing evidently wishes to lay emphasis upon the fact that all religions have certain true principles in common, to which alone they owe their vitality. But he could not possibly have wished to maintain that all the principles of the Jew, Moslem and Christian are equally true and of equal value in their application to practical life. In the same manner it might be maintained that the Episcopalian, Presbyterian and Roman Catholic all entertain certain essentially Christian principles, to which alone they owe their strength, while they allow other tenets of altogether inferior practical importance to split them up into distinct Christian bodies. But even these need not prevent their being regarded as together constituting the Christian Church, nor interfere with such legislation on the part of the state, as would give them equal privileges and protection.

On the morning of the 15th June we were supposed to be within sight of land and not far off New York, but we were lying in the midst of a thick fog, with engines at rest. At noon it cleared up beautifully, and in the afternoon the "Andes" steamed into the harbour of New York. In a few hours afterwards its passengers were dispersed through the great city, whose life and bustle seemed eminently fitted for driving from the mind all the scenes and impressions of the past few weeks, and even months. Bullethead and I happened to choose the same hotel, and made an engagement to meet each other at the Centennial Exhibition, which both of us were bent on visiting.

The ride next day from New York to Philadelphia was but a step, considering the distances I had recently trversed, and, from nature's grandeur in all its forms, the transition to the magnificence of Art in the Exhibition came quite as a matter of course. It was almost bewildering to me to visit there the countries of Central and South America, some of which I had just seen, and to find out after all how ignorant I was concerning them; how little I knew about the ancient pottery of Peru, or the minerals of Mexico. I searched through between them and as far as Brazil and the Argentine Republic, without discovering any trace of Ecuador, which, I afterwards found, had not "participated" in the Exhibition. It had not, with all its natural riches, mustered up money or courage enough to send a bag of coffee or a piece of pumice stone, while Norway, with sterile soil and inhospitable climate, but energetic and Protestant people had made the most valuable and interesting contributions. To walk through the Norwegian Court was the next best thing to revisiting a country where I had spent some of the happiest years of my life. The wood carvings, silver ornaments, the carioles, or small gigs, and even the blocks of minerals were continually awakening in my mind recollections of incidents and scenes nearly twenty years old. As in duty bound, my next visit was to Canada, and my national pride was gratified on beholding her splendid contributions, as well as those from Great Britain and her other colonies and dependencies.

Next day, the 17th June, I spent wholly in the Main Exhibition Building, Machinery Hall, Judges Hall, and U. S. Government collections, in search of specially interesting exhibits, and also waiting on a few of the many notable men whom the Exhibition had drawn together.

The 18th June was a Sunday, and the Exhibition was closed. Bullethead, who had arrived the previous day, did not fail to express his disgust, nor I my satisfaction, and I remarked to him :

"'This decision of the Centennial Commissioners is a "great victory for the Christian party."

" What party is that?" asked Mr. Bullethead.

" The one you ought to belong to if you are a Republican."

" Do you mean 'the God in the constitution party'?"

" That was its earlier name, but now it is represented by " the National Reform Association, and is 'devoted to the " maintenance of the Sabbath laws, the Bible in the common " schools, the Christian law of marriage, and other Christian " features of the U. S. Government.'"

" But they want another amendment to the constitution?"

" Yes, such a 'religious amendment as will indicate that " the United States is a Christian nation, and place all its " Christian laws, institutions and usages on an undeniable " legal basis in the very charter of the Government.'"

" Well, I think they are giving themselves a great deal of "unnecessary trouble."

" Why?"

" Because all these things will take care of themselves."

" A great many farseeing and pious men in your country " do not think so, and if your party, the Republican, were " wise, or even worldly wise, it would take up this very " matter into its platform."

"The Republican party can't afford to do so just now."

" Well, in a few years the question, 'Is this a Christian " Nation,' will have to be answered. It is being asked " very frequently now."

" But what is the use of all this fuss. Will their amend-" ment make people any better?"

" In the long run it will have that tendency," answered I.

" Yes, I fear it will be after a very long run," retorted Bullethead.

" It will keep the Bible in the national schools and " preserve the religious character which they undoubtedly " had originally."

" But can the mere reading of the Bible materially " improve the character of the scholars and the nation ?"

" The Bible is the only existing text book by which the " human heart can be disciplined," I maintained, " and it " would serve as an instrument whereby the teacher might, " if so minded, better enforce the principles of unsectarian " religion, virtue and morality."

" Yes, ' if so minded,' " said Bul'ethead, " but that is " none of his business; that must be left to the parents " and the parsons."

" But," said I, " the 'Liberal League' which has been " organised in Boston, will not allow the parsons, and " scarcely the parents, to have anything to do with it."

I then explained to Bullethead the "Demands of Liberalism," as they are given in the *Index*, an avowedly atheistical newspaper. The Liberals, or rather " Libertines," (as they were called in Calvin's day), demand " that all religious services now sustained by the Govern- " ment shall be abolished, and especially that the use of the " Bible in the public schools, whether ostensibly as a text " book, or avowedly as a book of religious worship, shall " be prohibited. We demand that all laws looking to the " enforcement of Christian morality shall be abrogated, and " that all laws shall be conformed to the requirements of " natural morality, equal rights and impartial liberty." How history repeats itself! This sounds like the language of the French Convention in 1793, and the libertines, "requirements of natural morality" corresponds to Danton's "Worship of Reason." All this would be very discouraging, were it not that, among the Americans, to recognize an evil and to provide a remedy are, historically speaking, almost simultaneous operations.

Bullethead's proposal to leave religious education to the parsons seems after all to be the true cure, and the more we consider the matter, the more does it appear evident that clergymen are at fault. Of course, in the rearing of every family, the parents up to a certain point undertake the education of their children in all particulars. By education is meant the general development of the individual in body, heart and mind. The parents are chiefly concerned for the nourishment and health of the body, and have but little time usually for disciplining the hearts of their children, inculcating obedience, justice, unselfishness, purity, and love, and eradicating all the wickedness which is truly said to reside naturally in the human heart. They can as little do this as attend to the education of the minds of their children. But while the charge of their mental instruction is duly committed to and imparted by the teacher, and the intellect, understanding, reason or judgment duly cultivated by him, the duty of disciplining the heart is not transferred in a similar formal and well-understood manner from the parents to the clergymen. The consequence is that it is to a frightful extent neglected, and, in the best cases, receives only a slight attention for a couple of hours on Sunday. It is not supposed, on this theory, that parents, teachers and clergymen have each their well-defined and quite distinct spheres of labour, for the various parts of the individual seemed to be dove-tailed into each other, and so must the various schools for educating them overlap each other's boundaries. But it seems plain that while our teachers are under-paid and over-worked, our clergymen, although certainly not over-paid, have abundance of time to attend more thoroughly to the training of the rising generation in "righteousness and true holiness."

An approach to such a system of training exists at present in Scandinavia. In Norway, for instance, Lutheranism is the state religion, and the "church department" as much a part of the government machinery there as is the British "War Office" in England. But the state is supreme, and the "church department" has a minister in charge of it just in the same manner as our Department of Customs. The Bishop of Agershuns, a sort of Metropolitan, is this minister, and at the same time a member of the government. The bishops, "provsts," parish priests, pastors and "capellans" under him are simultaneously government officers and officers of the church. They are paid by the state and have very onerous duties to perform; returns to make to government, registers of births, deaths and marriages to keep, besides performing the duties belonging to their more sacred office. Among the latter, one of the most important is the training of candidates for confirmation. None are admitted to it who cannot both read and write, and the pastor instructs regularly his class of candidates in "religion" with a diligence that would put our clergymen of all denominations to shame. No one thinks of going out to service, or applying for a situation, who cannot produce her or his certificate of confirmation. Then, the common schools are regularly visited by the clergyman, who consults with the school-master as to the character and qualifications of the various pupils and the best means of pushing them on to confirmation. But, for all this, it must be stated that "a loyal opposition" to this established church would be a God-send. Formalism and inertness frequently prevail.

Promotion is sometimes of more interest to the clergyman than the cure of souls. Among much that is encouraging and praiseworthy there is a frequent dearth of earnestness among these "spiritual pastors." Nor does the tree bring forth unimpeachable fruit. The better classes are indeed honest, kind, hospitable and cultivated, but among the common people the youth of both sexes are not always exemplary in their conduct. Drunkenness prevails among the men, and the women are rather lax as regards their notions of virtue. That I do not exaggerate the latter circumstance is proved by the presence among the beautiful national music of Norway, of an exquisitely plaintive song called "*Ifjor gjet eg Gjeita,*" of which I translate the following verse :

"A year ago I tended goats,
"In the valley dark and deepest,
"Now upon my aching heart,
"Thou, baby mine, unconscious sleepest;
"A year ago I was seventeen,
"And courted by the proudest swain ;
"But now I'm old before my time,
"And food for jesting and disdain."

When the Vikings of old issued from the northern fjords and ravaged mercilessly and fought valiantly on more southern soils, they were besouled by their belief in Valhalla and the bliss that there awaited those who died in fight. Let us hope that a revival of some sort may yet infuse into the Christianity of our own day at least as much faith and vigour as exhibited themselves in the false religion of these sturdy old pagans. From them, at any rate, we can learn that a false religion, thoroughly believed in, is better than none at all for vigorous national life.

The Scottish Education Act of 1872 contains a provision (already cited, p. 175) for the religious instruction of the young, which will probably turn out to be the germ of a better educational system hereafter. It provides a time during which "religious observances may be practised and " religious instruction given," and enacts that it " shall be " specified in a table approved of by the Scotch Education " Department." It is to be hoped that the people and clergy of Scotland will take advantage of the opportunity thus afforded them, and make adequate provision for the spiritual discipline of the young. In this way state, church and family might be brought each to do their duty as essential parts of a great engine, and Scotland might be able to prove to the world in the future, as she has done in the past, that " Righteousness exalteth a nation." The great obstacle to this, however, will probably be the theory which Scotch theologians maintain as to the respective spheres of church and state. They will probably insist upon the Presbyterian principle that they are " co-ordinate jurisdictions, each supreme in its own affairs." This would place the Scotch Kirk in the position of a strong-minded wife, very tenacious of woman's rights, although not going quite so far as to " wear the breeks," a fault of which she was very guilty in earlier days.

On the morning of the 19th June, I parted from Bullethead, rapidly reached New York, passed as rapidly through it, and on the morning of the 20th found myself in Montreal, after having been absent three months and two days, and travelled a distance of over 12,000 miles. I had left Canada completely enveloped in her snow mantle, and I returned in the breathing-space which follows seed-time, when she was clothed in all the beauty of her summer dress. To me she appeared inexpressibly beautiful, and, if less gorgeously attired than the regions of the South, far more chaste and dignified. I was thankful to be at home again, and had not the slightest hankering after any of the enticing scenes

I had visited. I rather thought it to be my duty, as I believe it to be that of our whole community, to "thank the " Lord for the good land which he has given us."

But, although it is the duty of the people of Canada to thank Almighty God for mere material resources, and for the circumstance that these are of such a nature as to draw out and properly develope our physical energies, we ought not to forget that we have been blessed with many moral and religious advantages for which we cannot be too thankful. Furthermore these ought not not to be allowed to lie dormant, but should be so improved as to bring forth the best of fruit. "By their fruits shall ye know them," and by the results of our church and school systems must they be judged. Do our "sons grow up as the young plants " and our daughters as the polished corners of the temple?" Do they not rather seem to have learnt that "man's chief " end " is not to "glorify God," but to have "a good time," and to enjoy *that* as long as possible, if not quite "for ever?" Are our maidens modest and virtuous; our young men brave and honest? If we cannot answer these questions satisfactorily and without hesitation, then something must have been amiss with their education. This is in our day becoming more and more the work of the state, which justifies its interference on the ground that education is essential to the production of a good member of society, and that a large proportion of the heads of families neglect to furnish it to their children. This reasoning is doubtless correct, provided education is understood to mean the development of the whole individual and of all his faculties and powers. So far, however, the state has been mainly concerned regarding the intellectual instruction of the young, while their physical training on the one hand, and the cultivation of their moral and religious natures on the other, have been comparatively neglected. And, strange to say, large and influential bodies of Christians justify this state of things, and maintain that common or national schools ought to be "unsectarian," or non-religious! But such schools cannot eliminate religion from their teaching without inculcating atheism ; this ignoring of religion fosters practical infidelity. Our laws are founded on Christianity, our legislation guided by it, and yet we neglect or refuse to allow it to mould our educational system, or cause our children to be systematically taught its precepts! Nationally we disobey the command, "And thou shalt teach them diligently " unto thy children," and we deny Him before men whose teaching alone can exalt us as a nation. Let us beware of looking around us and finding out the faults of other nations, saying practically at the same time, " I am holier than thou." In Canada, just as much as in other countries, how to secure the blessing of a national system of religious education, and at the same time be just to the individual citizen, and even considerate and tender to his religious prejudices, is the problem of the day. Although in this Dominion we have or ought to have no established church, there is no doubt about our having a national religion. We profess to be Christians, to believe in a King of kings and Lord of lords, whose providence is a substantial thing, and without whose teachings our children would make but sorry members of society. All this we profess privately, but when it comes to speaking as a nation, we are silent. Our Union Act contains as little reference to the Almighty Ruler of the Universe as does the Constitution of the United States, and for fear of offending man and his religious " views " we hesitate not to ignore entirely the Creator.* This omission may not, however, be so important

---

* Since this was written the Dominion House of Commons has decided to open its sessions by prayer.

as it seems, for, unlike that of the United States, our fundamental law is unwritten, and our sovereign is VICTORIA, *by the Grace of God, Queen, Defender of the Faith.* Let us be thankful that these few words enable us to maintain, what we are too likely to forget, that our highest ruler claims under the British Constitution to be the "minister of God."

The real question for us, and for every other Christian nation, is, however, this: Can we not acknowledge God, especially as the source of all human authority, and make systematic, legal and sufficient provision for His worship without doing injustice to, or infringing on, the rights of the individual citizen? It would seem to be quite possible. The British North America or Union Act of 1867 authorizes the Queen, Senate and House of Commons "to " make laws for the peace, order and good government of " Canada, in relation to all matters not coming within the " class of subjects by this Act assigned exclusively to the " Legislatures of the Provinces." Now, although education is included in the class of subjects referred to, national religion is not. It would therefore seem fully competent for the Dominion Parliament to legislate somewhat in this strain: Whereas this is a Christian nation; whereas we acknowledge Almighty God, and whereas it is expedient to make better arrangements than heretofore for His public worship, and for training the people of this Dominion in the practice of the Christian religion: Be it therefore enacted: that in the valuation roll of each municipality shall be set down the religious persuasion of each land or property holder; that it shall be lawful for the council of each municipality, if they see fit, to impose a tax, not exceeding a certain rate, for church purposes; that it shall be the duty of each municipal treasurer, on receipt of the taxes so imposed, to pay over the amount levied on each ratepayer to the legal representative of the religious denomination to which he belongs. In some such way as this a properly organized system of supporting our churches might take the place of the voluntaryism now prevalent without doing injustice to any individual. The same principle is at present in force and works satisfactorily for the support of education in the Province of Quebec. It of course tends to the establishment of denominational schools, but these might nevertheless, and ought, to a certain extent, to be placed under the control and subject to the inspection of the State. So far, we have not been obliged, in Canada, to legislate concerning the support of the poor, but we cannot long expect to be so favored. The principle above explained might also be extended, when the necessity arises, to the support of the poor of the various communions, now to such a large extent provided for in an unsystematic, and therefore possibly expensive manner, by private charity. Of course, the highest talent, the most profound statesmanship, the most unimpeachable disinterestedness, and the most undeviating candour and openness will be required in devising a satisfactory law for accomplishing these objects, and in framing its details, but the matter will sooner or later have to be studied and legislated on, and in the end the Christian Church recognized as the honoured consort of the State, able and willing to do her part in training up for it diligent, conscientious and patriotic subjects, and as forming with these and with the state, a model *nation*, making its steady advances with other human institutions on the road to perfection.

Of all parts of the Dominion, the one in which the ground seems best prepared for a discussion and settlement of these questions is, without doubt, the Province of Quebec.

The fundamental idea of the predominating Roman Catholic population as regards education seems to be that a purely secular training is worse than none, and, in all likelihood, it will not take very much study on the part of the Protestant element, when it once brings its mind to bear on the subject, to convince it that the Roman Catholic principle in this respect is not far wrong. And, further, a great many circumstances and occurrences are forcing upon the public the consideration of the question as to what really is the connection which ought to be permitted to exist betwixt Church and State in this Province. It is a melancholy reflection that eighteen centuries of history and statesmanship have not sufficed to answer this question, and it is rather mortifying to find it turning up in our own day and in our own country demanding a settlement. It is for us boldly to grapple with it, furnish the answer, and set it at rest for ever. If we do, then will Quebec, instead of being regarded as a few centuries behind the rest of the world, instead of being looked upon as a strayed or misplaced piece of medieval Europe, take the proud position of having been the first to set its house in order, and be able to give a lesson in political economy, and an example in statesmanship, to other nations not only lying near the route "To the Andes," but scattered over the face of the whole earth.

www.ingramcontent.com/pod-product-compliance
Lightning Source LLC
Chambersburg PA
CBHW020247170426
43202CB00008B/257